"I would recommend *Helping Your Child with OCD* to anyone caring for a child with OCD. It can easily be adapted to group homes, multi-generational families, and recreational settings. This workbook is written in an easy-to-follow style that helps the layperson to grasp the concepts—even if they are in crisis! Thank you for providing this very useful workbook."

—Wendy Birkhan, BSW, RSW, social work therapist, OCD and the Family, Ottawa, Ontario; her own immediate family includes four people living with OCD

"*Helping Your Child with OCD* is an easy-to-read, practical guide for parents of children with OCD. This workbook covers all of the most commonly asked questions and will assist many parents who struggle with the day-to-day challenges posed by their child's OCD symptoms. Fitzgibbons and Pedrick offer hope and therapeutic strategies to families in need of this resource."

—Barbara Van Noppen, Ph.D., Brown University Department of Psychiatry

"*Helping Your Child with OCD* goes beyond other self help books for parents. Besides offering parents a thoughtful plan of action to help their suffering children, it provides a way for them to understand what their child is going through. It also focuses on the kinds of changes parents will need to make in their own lives. This will enable parents to be effective 'coaches' as well as improve the quality of their lives."

—Jonathan Grayson, Ph.D., Director, Anxiety & Agoraphobia Treatment Center, Bala Cynwyd, Pennsylvania

"Whenever I hear from parents of a child with OCD, I experience a spasm of sadness. How can they help their child? Fortunately, this workbook is available. It offers helpful suggestions on a range of topics, including guidelines on how to interact with professionals working with your child and worksheets to help keep track of what is going on. It is an important resource every parent dealing with a child with OCD needs."

—James M. Claiborn, Ph.D., ABPP, psychologist and author of *The Habit Change Workbook* and *The BDD Workbook*

"Lee Fitzgibbons' work is well grounded in cognitive behavioral theory, yet she is an excellent teacher who is particularly adept at conveying complex theoretical concepts to patients in a clear and concise way. Nowhere is this strength more evident than in her work with children and adolescents. *Helping Your Child with OCD* includes the kind of practical, hands-on advice that she is so skilled at giving. It will serve as a foundation for helping children get and stay better."

—Martin Franklin, Ph.D., Assistant Professor of Clinical Psychology in Psychiatry and Clinical Director of the Center for the Treatment and Study of Anxiety at the University of Pennsylvania School of Medicine

Helping Your Child *with* OCD

A WORKBOOK FOR PARENTS OF CHILDREN WITH OBSESSIVE-COMPULSIVE DISORDER

Lee Fitzgibbons, Ph.D.,
and Cherry Pedrick, RN

NEW HARBINGER PUBLICATIONS, INC.

Publisher's Note

This publication is designed to provide accurate and authoritative information in regard to the subject matter covered. It is sold with the understanding that the publisher is not engaged in rendering psychological, financial, legal, or other professional services. If expert assistance or counseling is needed, the services of a competent professional should be sought.

Distributed in Canada by Raincoast Books

Copyright © 2003 by Lee Fitzgibbons and Cherry Pedrick
New Harbinger Publications, Inc.
5674 Shattuck Avenue
Oakland, CA 94609

Cover design by Poulson/Gluck
Edited by Karen O'Donnell Stein
Text design by Tracy Marie Carlson

ISBN-10 1-57224-332-5
ISBN-13 978-1-57224-332-3

All Rights Reserved

Printed in the United States of America

New Harbinger Publications' Web site address: www.newharbinger.com

08   07   06

10   9   8   7   6   5   4   3   2

Contents

Part III

What the Parent Can Do

Acknowledgements

Lee Fitzgibbons, Ph.D.

First, I want to thank and acknowledge all of the people who have taught me both directly or indirectly how to help people with OCD. I began working with people who had OCD at the Center for the Treatment and Study of Anxiety (currently located at the University of Pennsylvania) where I was mentored by Drs. Edna Foa, Michael Kozak, and Martin Franklin. I learned from and worked with them for close to five years, and I am indebted to them both for transforming me into a cognitive behavioral therapist (with emphasis on behavioral) and for developing my competence in treating OCD. For the next five years, I worked at the Anxiety and Agoraphobia Treatment Center in Bala Cynwyd, PA, as the director of their Children's Program. I learned from all of my colleagues there and benefited from being a member of a smart, supportive, and loving work family. However, my work at the AATC was particularly wonderful because it allowed me to work with Dr. Jon Grayson. Association with him has opened many doors to me, including the opportunity to write this book with Cherry Pedrick. Because of him, I had opportunities to assist on camping trips for people with OCD, to assist at the biweekly meetings of the Philadelphia "G.O.A.L." Support Group, and to discuss treatment strategies during weekly peer supervision. He promoted my career by pushing me to present at national conferences when I had no inclination to do so. Besides being a fine mentor and very decent human being, Dr. Grayson is a gifted clinician. He has a talent for helping people to understand what it feels like to struggle with OCD, for finding metaphors to help people understand their own struggle, and for finding creative strategies to move them to change. His ideas are sprinkled liberally throughout this book. While I have attempted to adequately cite him, I fear that these citations may still fall short of his actual contribution because his thinking has so profoundly influenced my own. It is hard to know where his thoughts about treatment end and mine begin. A special thanks is also extended to my colleague at AATC, Kathleen Parrish, M.A., M.S., with whom I have had the privilege of doing many workshops over the years and whose creative lyrics consistently amaze me— thank you for letting me include your song at the end. I would also like to acknowledge my indebtedness to other authors, whose work I have devoured and draw on daily: most importantly, the work of Drs. John March, Tamar Chansky, and Aureen Pinto Wagner. Hopefully, you will be the benefactors of the gifts of all these talented people.

Next, on a more personal level, I also wish to thank my parents whose willingness to drop everything to help take care of my daughter was unbelievably generous. Truly, this book would not have been finished without their help, as it allowed me to actually sit down to write. Lastly, I would like to thank and acknowledge my husband, Dr. Gordon Street, for so many things. He cheerfully picked up slack. He absorbed my writing crankiness without retaliating or feeling hurt. He believed in me and encouraged me when I felt discouraged. He let me disappear for long periods of time without complaint. But most importantly, he provided me with crucial editorial assistance. Whenever I wrote myself into a box with terribly muddled thinking, he tromped through my ideas and helped me find clarity. His assistance definitely improved my contributions to the book. Finally, I heartfully thank Cherry Pedrick (and New Harbinger) for approaching me to coauthor this book with her. I am grateful for the opportunity she provided, the expertise she contributed, and the good humor she managed to demonstrate throughout the entire process.

Cherry Pedrick, RN

I am grateful to my husband Jim and son James for the encouragement and support they provided throughout the process of writing this book. I'm thankful to Dr. Michael Jenike, to whom I often turn for the latest information. Most of all, I thank my God for making it all possible. I have been fascinated by Lee Fitzgibbons' ingenious way of helping parents deal with their child's OCD. It has been an honor to help her shape her ideas into a very useful workbook.

We both thank our editor Karen O'Donnel Stein, who made the book much more concise and clear. She encouraged us to make challenging concepts more understandable. We also thank Tesilya Hanauer and all the others at New Harbinger Publications who made this book a reality.

Introduction

Do you have a child who constantly checks things, washes and cleans, or can't go through a door without touching the sides? Is his or her behavior causing great distress and interfering with functioning at home or school? If so, your child could have obsessive-compulsive disorder (OCD), an anxiety disorder that can rob children of the joy and fun that should be a part of every child's life.

If your child is struggling with these symptoms, do not despair. While twenty years ago there seemed to be little hope for individuals with this disorder, today the situation has changed. Mental health professionals and scientists have made tremendous strides in developing treatments and medications that alleviate the symptoms of OCD. Now, more than ever before, there is reason for hope that children can overcome OCD.

The goal of this book is to provide help for families of children ages six through eighteen and even beyond who are struggling with OCD. Facing obsessive-compulsive disorder is essential to your child's mental health. Unattended, OCD can seem like a huge, scary monster at the very core of your child's and family's life. It does not need to remain front and center. When your child and your family learn how to handle it, OCD can become merely a nagging nuisance that does not need to be feared. *Helping Your Child with OCD* will give you strategies for helping your child put OCD in its proper place—a place of insignificance—so that your child and family can be in control once again.

How This Book Can Help You

Helping Your Child with OCD is not intended to be a substitute for psychiatric or psychological treatment by a qualified mental health professional. Rather, it should be used in the following ways:

◆ As an adjunct to treatment by a professional. *Helping Your Child with OCD* can assist a therapist in his or her role of coach, guide, and adviser as you and the therapist help your child gain control over OCD.

◆ As a source of information for people who have not yet sought professional help. Reading this book can help you learn as much about OCD as possible. In the process you may determine that the obsessive-compulsive behaviors your child exhibits are part of normal development, or that they signify the beginning of OCD and a need for treatment.

◆ By assisting family members and mental health professionals who seek a better understanding of OCD. *Helping Your Child with OCD* can assist you as you provide support to those struggling with OCD.

◆ By assisting parents of children who display obsessive-compulsive behaviors that don't approach the severity of full-fledged OCD.

Helping Your Child with OCD is divided into three parts. Part I will help you to understand OCD, its diagnosis, its symptoms, and the most widely accepted theories about its causes. Part II will cover the various treatment options and help you decide which ones are best for your child. Part III, the core of this book, will help you understand what you can realistically do to help your child and family deal with OCD.

From the Authors

Lee Fitzgibbons, Ph.D.

Hi. Thank you for picking up this book. I think that reading this book represents real courage on your part—the courage to recognize that there may be a problem that needs your attention and the courage to contemplate doing something about it. I hope that together we can make a real difference in your child's life.

People often ask me why I work with people with OCD. I work with people who have OCD simply because I really like them. When I stand in a room full of people with OCD, I cannot help but realize what tremendous people they are. The very qualities I value most are the qualities that make people vulnerable to OCD: intelligence, creativity, honesty, and a huge capacity to care for other people. Helping such people, particularly children, is tremendously rewarding. So, while I do not live with OCD in my own life, I do have the understanding that comes from having accompanied numerous children and adults as they wrested control of their life from OCD. I am grateful to all of these individuals and their families for sharing their lives, their struggles, and their victories. These people have taught me, shaped me, and inspired me.

Cherry Pedrick, RN

After twenty years working as a registered nurse, I made a career change. In 1995, I took up mouse and keyboard to pursue a writing career. I wrote articles for several magazines, then I coauthored *The OCD Workbook* with Bruce M. Hyman, Ph.D., in 1999. I coauthored *The Habit Change Workbook* and *The BDD Workbook* with James Claiborn, Ph.D. My interest in cognitive behavioral therapy began when I used its principles in the treatment of my own OCD. Over the years, I've met many families struggling with OCD. I am grateful for the opportunity to assist Dr. Fitzgibbons in bringing forth the latest information about treatment and support to parents of children with OCD.

Part I

Does My Child Have OCD?

You may already know the answer to this question. Perhaps your child was diagnosed with obsessive-compulsive disorder (OCD) years ago. You may be satisfied with the treatment your child is receiving, but you are reading this book because you want to learn as much as you can about OCD so you and your family can provide more support. Or perhaps the treatment your child is receiving does not seem to be working, and you want to learn why and how to help. Perhaps your child has not been diagnosed with OCD but you suspect that he or she has the disorder. You might not be clear about what OCD is, much less what the treatment should be or what you can do to help your child, and you want to learn more.

In part 1, we'll cover the basics: What is OCD? What types of OCD are there? What looks like OCD but isn't? What is the impact of OCD on both the child and the family? In chapter 1, we will explain the cycle of uncertainty that drives OCD. We suggest that you read the chapter through even if you are quite familiar with OCD, because we may present some ideas that are new to you. In chapter 2, we will help you unmask your child's OC (obsessive-compulsive) symptoms. We'll help you recognize behaviors that are sometimes confused with OCD, but are not. We'll review the diverse obsessions and related compulsions that are OC symptoms. In chapter 3, we'll focus on the impact of OCD on your child and your family. To be fully supportive of your child, you'll need to have some understanding of what it *feels* like to have OCD. You'll learn to understand how your child feels and how OCD affects your family.

Chapter 1

What Is OCD?

Cases of OCD have been described since the fourteenth century. The disorder has been called religious melancholy, perfectionism, petrifaction of the psyche, the demonic condition, obsessive doubting, compulsion neurosis, and obsessive neurosis. Sigmund Freud believed OCD was caused by subconscious conflicts, but his theories never resulted in effective treatments. In recent years, researchers pursuing other theories have developed effective treatments, and their work has increased our understanding of the disorder and its origin.

Let's take a look at the definition of OCD in the manual used by mental health professionals in the United States, the *Diagnostic and Statistical Manual of Mental Disorders,* fourth edition *(DSM-IV-TR).* It states:

> The essential features of Obsessive-Compulsive Disorder are recurrent obsessions or compulsions that are severe enough to be time consuming (i.e., they take more than one hour a day) or cause marked distress or significant impairment. At some point during the course of the disorder, the person has recognized that the obsessions or compulsions are excessive or unreasonable. (APA 2000, 456-457)

Notice that this definition has four essential components. First, in order to warrant receiving a diagnosis of OCD, a person must have either obsessions or compulsions (although most people with OCD have both). Second, these obsessions or compulsions must be recurrent (they happen repeatedly). Third, these obsessions or compulsions must cause problems for the person, either causing dysfunction (consuming a lot of time or significantly impairing the person's ability to work, learn, or have relationships) or marked distress, or both. Fourth, the person is not delusional (he or she does not unshakably believe that the obsessional concerns are realistic or that the compulsions are absolutely necessary).

To understand this definition (and to understand the child with OCD), it is essential to understand what obsessions and compulsions are, including how they differ both from each other and from normal thoughts and behaviors. These distinctions are not as simple as they might seem and are sometimes difficult even for OCD experts to make.

Obsessions are intrusive, recurring, persistent thoughts (impulses, ideas, images, or feelings) that cause excessive anxiety and distress. It is not just that the thoughts are unwanted, often make little sense to the person, and are experienced as difficult to dismiss or disregard; to be called obsessions these thoughts must cause anxiety or distress. Consider the advertising jingle or children's song that gets stuck in your mind for a while. Taken alone, such a thought would not be considered an obsession, because it would not ordinarily be accompanied by distress or anxiety. However, if the same jingle were recurrent and intrusive and caused marked distress or anxiety, it would then be an obsession. With an obsession, distress is the brain's alarm indicating that something is not right or that something bad may happen.

Compulsions are purposeful and repetitive behaviors that are performed in order to relieve, neutralize (undo), or prevent the anxiety or distress caused by obsessions, restoring a sense of safety. As such they can be considered *neutralizing* or *safety* behaviors. So, compulsions are not intrusive, because they are not involuntary. They may seem intrusive or out of control to someone who has had OCD for a while, but they are in fact intentional. Compulsions are not just physical behaviors (such as repeatedly checking light switches), but can also be mental behaviors, words, thoughts, or ideas that the person with OCD thinks to him- or herself in order to prevent, neutralize, or relieve anxiety.

One more important concept, which is not mentioned in the official diagnostic criteria, is *avoidance*. Like compulsions, avoidance is a neutralizing or safety behavior. Avoidance is a behavior done to ensure or restore a sense of safety by maneuvering around a potential threat. Generally, as time elapses, people with OCD notice what situations trigger their obsessions. Their preferred method of dealing with OCD anxiety related to the obsessions is often to avoid these difficult situations in the first place. Avoidance is generally a sufferer's preferred response for many reasons. It's often easy to do, especially early in the course of the disorder. It is also easily hidden or can frequently be excused as a personal preference; for example, avoiding restaurant food that might be contaminated because of poor worker hygiene can be excused with the statement "I prefer home-cooked meals to restaurant food." Lastly, avoidance circumvents the perceived need to complete effortful, time-consuming, and sometimes embarrassing rituals, because when the triggers are avoided there is no distress to prompt compulsions.

Obsessive-compulsive disorder is considered a *neurobehavioral disorder,* meaning that part of the problem is due to the physical makeup of the brain and part of the problem is due to the person's behavioral responses. (As a disorder that has a strong biological component, it's a "no-fault" disorder.) If your child has this disorder, it's not your fault or anyone else's. In people with OCD there appears to be a neurological "glitch" that makes an individual more sensitive or reactive to potential danger. This glitch makes it more difficult for a person to dismiss danger warnings, even when these warnings are false alarms. Experiencing these alarms leads to behavior aimed at avoiding or reducing distress. These actions feed back and make the alarms seem more believable. We call this "the cycle of uncertainty."

Understanding the Cycle of Uncertainty

Our discussion of the cycle of uncertainty is largely based on the ideas of Jon Grayson, Ph.D., a friend and colleague of Dr. Fitzgibbons who has strongly influenced her understanding of OCD. One way of thinking about the brain glitch discussed above is that people with OCD have a lower tolerance for uncertainty (Grayson 1996, 1999). The possibility of danger, however unlikely, leads to "false alarms" or obsessions. To reduce the risk of harm or alarm, the person with OCD engages in compulsions and avoidance. Avoidance and compulsions are safety or neutralizing behaviors that become part of the problem for three reasons. First, responding with avoidance or compulsions strengthens that behavioral response and makes it more likely to recur because the safety or neutralizing behavior has been practiced and reinforced. Second, the avoidance or compulsion at first appears to work and is thus confirmed as "necessary." Safety experienced—the absence of predicted disaster or the feeling of being safe—is wrongly attributed to the safety or neutralizing behavior rather than to the more probable explanation that there was little danger to begin with. Third, because of the person's intolerance for uncertainty, the safety or neutralizing behavior intended to address the problem does not continue to work. Doubt and anxiety return, necessitating more safety or neutralizing behaviors to ensure or restore relief. The cycle repeats and worsens.

Let's examine some of the components of this cycle more closely. The intrusive thoughts of OCD are not the core of the underlying problem. Studies have shown that people without OCD have the same kinds of intrusive, negative thoughts that constitute the obsessions of OCD. People without OCD easily dismiss these intrusions without a second thought. However, the lower tolerance for uncertainty in people with OCD means that to them these thoughts *feel* true: The thought that a doorknob *might* be contaminated by infectious blood feels like "That doorknob is contaminated with infectious blood!" The thought "Maybe I'll stab someone with that knife" feels like "Oh, no! I'm going to stab someone with that knife!" It's as if merely thinking something bad will magically make it so. The point is that the person thinking these thoughts experiences them as realities or premonitions and, as such, they take on a loaded significance. As a result, the thoughts are far more disturbing than they would be to a person without OCD.

The distress is so extreme and unpleasant that the person devises various coping responses in order to manage the distress and perceived risks. As we have mentioned, two kinds of neutralizing or safety behaviors develop, avoidance and compulsions. Avoidance can be separated into two behaviors: behavioral avoidance and mental avoidance (thought suppression). Both forms follow from the assumption that if the person with OCD could simply avoid thinking the unwanted thoughts, then he or she wouldn't have to deal with the resulting feelings or perceived risks. For example, a person who suffers from violent obsessions will often engage in mental avoidance by trying to think only gentle thoughts and by trying to block violent thoughts. If the person notices a violent thought forming, he or she will try to stop thinking that thought and will deliberately think about something else. Such a person might also engage in behavioral avoidance and try not to use knives, avoid watching news programs in which violent behavior might be reported, or stay away from movies that might contain violent material. Behavioral avoidance can support mental avoidance because it minimizes exposure to situations and things that elicit obsessions. Behavioral avoidance can also be intended to reduce perceived risk. In the example above, not using knives reduces the likelihood of experiencing an obsession and also eliminates the risk of impulsively stabbing someone with a knife. While these responses, which stem from the ideas "If it makes you feel bad, don't think about it" and "If you think it's dangerous, don't do it," make logical sense, they actually increase the problem.

One of the most important concepts for you to master is "Avoidance always strengthens fear." Why? There are many reasons. First, practicing any behavior makes it stronger, especially if the behavior seems to produce a wanted outcome, so practicing avoidance makes the avoidant response stronger. Second, choosing to avoid something suggests that there must be a good reason to do so, so each choice to avoid something strengthens the belief that the false alarm is true. Third, avoidance blocks opportunities to disconfirm the need for fear, so the absence of disconfirming information is taken as confirmation that the alarm is real.

Avoidance breeds future avoidance partly because it appears to work in the short term. For example, if a person with OCD has obsessions about getting contaminated or sick from touching public surfaces such as doorknobs or public phones, it is likely that the person will avoid touching public surfaces as much as possible. This reduces the frequency of encountering possible germs and feeling contaminated and helps to keep anxiety low. Avoidance might actually increase the probability of staying healthy and, since the person does not get sick, he or she believes the avoidance is working. So, these behaviors appear effective. The more the person engages in the avoidance, the more he or she believes avoidance is necessary to maintain low anxiety and physical well-being. More importantly, the more the person exerts effort to avoid public surfaces, the more convinced he or she becomes that absolute certainty of safety, and vigilance to ensure it, are essential.

It may be clear why avoidance begets more avoidance, but how does it strengthen fear? Avoidance always strengthens fear because, as we mentioned above, the effort exerted to avoid the fearful situation validates the fear. The kicker is that, by engaging in avoidant behaviors consistently, the person with OCD never has the opportunity to experience situations and outcomes that would disconfirm their fears. The person never finds out what would happen if he or she did not practice avoidance. The person who does not touch public phones and doorknobs never challenges his or her fear and never discovers that he or she can get through an uncertain or fearful situation or remain healthy even after touching other people's germs. The person attributes safety to avoidance rather than to the correct reason, which the person might have understood if he or she had confronted the fearful situation—that the risk was relatively low in the first place.

The other avoidant strategy, mental avoidance, or thought suppression, also worsens the problem. Unfortunately, trying to push a thought out of your mind nearly always ensures that the thought will get stuck in your mind. For example, take a moment and try not to think about a big, green rabbit standing behind you and eating your hair. Think about anything else, but don't think about that ferocious big, green rabbit! If you work at this, you may at first succeed. But, if you were to continue for several minutes, especially if something bad were to happen should you fail, you would probably notice that all you could think about were big, green rabbits. So, in effect, trying to not think a thought guarantees that you will only think it more.

Thought suppression does not work for two reasons. First, the attempt to suppress a thought actually requires activating that thought because some awareness of the thought is necessary for a person to actively ward it off. Second, when a thought evokes fear, attempting to avoid the thought strengthens that fear because, as already explained, avoidance always strengthens fear. The very act of attempting to avoid a thought gives it power and supports the belief that it is significant, dangerous, abhorrent, and unmanageable.

A final problem with avoidance strategies is that it is nearly impossible to use them consistently and still function. In normal, everyday functioning, some things cannot be avoided. As a result, the person with OCD feels forced to come up with other coping responses (compulsions, or neutralizing or safety behaviors) to use when avoidance is not possible.

Compulsions are neutralizing or safety behaviors intended to prevent disaster, avoid responsibility for harm, make things right, or just make the problem thoughts or feelings go away. Safety behaviors are not unreasonable actions by themselves; they would make sense if there were a real danger. Consider the following scenario: As you leave your house you have the thought that you may have left the coffee pot on. You think about your actions as you were getting ready to leave and say to yourself, "No, I really don't think I turned it off." So you go back in to check. This is not an unreasonable behavior; it's a sensible response to a concern.

So how does a low tolerance for uncertainty change this scenario? Most of the time, when people without OCD have these kinds of thoughts and make these decisions, they make the correct decision (or they make the incorrect decision but don't worry about it). But people with OCD usually find it very difficult to make and trust their decisions. Someone with OCD might stand at the door having the thought about the coffee pot, remember turning the pot off while saying good-bye, and then think, "But what if I didn't? Maybe that was yesterday. I'd better go back in to be sure." So the person may return to make sure, discovering that, yes, the coffee pot was off. Nevertheless, the person feels better for having taken the precaution. In fact, he or she may even feel that the action of checking magically ensured the desired outcome. Either way, on or off, the person has ensured his or her safety and comfort. This brings us to a very important point—as with avoidance, initially compulsions work to provide a sense of safety and relief. The action, if it's a one-time event, is at worst a harmless waste of time.

Unfortunately, in people with OCD compulsions rarely stop here. Before long, the compulsions diminish in effectiveness because of the sufferer's intolerance for uncertainty. Remember that the sufferer wants to be 100 percent certain that the risk is gone. Because that level of certainty is never attainable, doubts surface. "Did I clean (or check, or repeat) enough?" "Maybe I didn't do that; I just think I did." The distress is back and relentless. Gradually, the compulsions lose their power to provide as much relief and don't work for as long a period of time as they did previously. When the relief experienced is less than expected, a compulsion might be changed or repeated until sufficient relief is achieved. Thus, compulsions tend to grow and become more complicated, with the person chasing after an elusive feeling of relief that seems sure to come with the next ritual. It becomes necessary to check something or repeat an action in a particular way or a magical number of times until it "feels right."

Even to the person engaging in them, it usually becomes obvious that the compulsions are excessive, ineffective, and distressing. Rather than providing relief, performing compulsions eventually makes the person with OCD feel out of control and creates more anxiety. So why perform compulsions? There are two answers. The first is that the person sees no other means to obtain relief; there appears to be no other antidote to the distress other than doing the ritual. The second is that, however poorly the ritual may work in the long term, the person at one time got short-term relief by doing their ritual, so he or she continues to expect and hope for that same relief. This is why we refer to rituals as "sensible behaviors gone awry." Below, you can see the progression from intrusive thoughts to repeated compulsions with little relief of anxiety.

Who Gets OCD?

OCD often starts in childhood. About one in every hundred children gets OCD (Yaryura-Tobias and Neziroglu 1997), typically between ages nine and thirteen. About two-thirds of all people with OCD experience their first symptoms before age twenty-five (Niehaus and Stein 1997). In rare cases, symptoms can sometimes be seen in children as young as three years old.

OCD tends to develop earlier in boys than in girls. In younger children, boys with OCD symptoms outnumber girls three to two. Girls seem to have more washing compulsions and boys more checking compulsions. In teens and adults, the ratio of men to women is about equal. OCD symptoms are typically mild at first and gradually worsen. A sudden onset suggests an atypical course and cause (see discussion of PANDAS below). A minority of people with OCD can look back and identify a specific event that seemed to

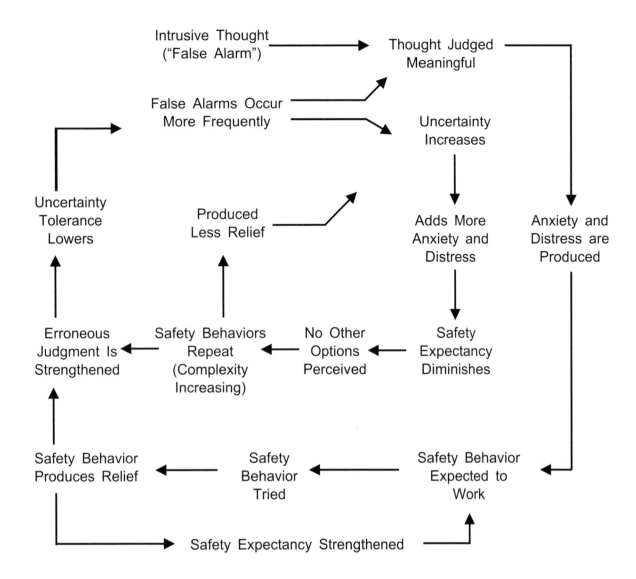

trigger the onset of their OCD. The vast majority of people with OCD can identify no trauma or difficult event when symptoms first occurred. Furthermore, research has not identified any common childhood experiences or parental practices that routinely result in the development of OCD. Thus, early theories that OCD resulted from trauma or bad parenting have not been supported. Rest assured, you did not cause your child's OCD; as we have said, a brain glitch is to blame.

What Causes OCD?

No one really knows for sure what causes OCD. Neuroimaging studies have indicated that the brains of people with OCD work differently than those of people without the disorder. Certain areas of the brain, which are critical in information processing, filtering and sorting sensory information, and generating emotions, appear to overfunction in individuals with OCD.

There also appears to be a chemical imbalance involved in OCD. Serotonin is an important neurotransmitter that seems to function inadequately in the brains of people who have OCD. This chemical messenger communicates between nerve cells, helping to control many biological processes, including mood, aggression, impulses, sleep, appetite, body temperature, and pain. Serotonin imbalance has also been identified as a contributing factor in depression, eating disorders, self-mutilation, and schizophrenia (Yaryura-Tobias and Neziroglu 1997).

Researchers are hard at work looking for a genetic cause of OCD. Most likely, a predisposition for OCD is caused by several genes, or perhaps several combinations of genes. Since 1930, researchers have reported finding obsessive-compulsive traits in the blood relatives of 20 to 40 percent of those studied. (Yaryura-Tobias and Neziroglu 1997). There appear to be higher rates of OCD, subclinical OCD (symptoms that aren't severe enough to warrant a diagnosis), Tourette's syndrome, and tics in relatives of people with OCD (Alsobrook and Pauls 1998). The occurrence of OCD traits in other family members appears to be more frequent for childhood-onset OCD than adult-onset OCD. Such observations suggest a stronger genetic link for childhood-onset OCD (Geller 1998).

Some research indicates that there are some nongenetic biological causes of OCD. These cases, however, are very rare; most cases of OCD occur without apparent cause other than heredity (Jenike 1998) with the exception of the type of childhood-onset OCD that sometimes develops in the months following a strep infection. This disorder is one manifestation of *pediatric autoimmune neuropsychiatric disorders associated with streptococcal infections* (PANDAS). Research on PANDAS is recent, and largely based on case studies, so conclusions about this etiology may be premature. Reports made thus far estimate that as many as 25 to 30 percent of childhood-onset OCD cases may be PANDAS-related.

PANDAS-related OCD generally develops in children age three to puberty, several months after a strep throat infection appears to have resolved. It is thought to result from damage to the basal ganglia area of the brain, sustained when antibodies produced by the body to fight the infection attack the child's own nervous system. PANDAS-related OCD typically has a sudden and severe onset. Often, other neuropsychiatric symptoms (tics, hyperactivity, heightened sensory sensitivity, irritability, mood changes, handwriting changes, loss of math skills, fidgeting, impulsivity, poor attention span, and separation anxiety) surface or worsen at the time the OCD symptoms begin.

Prevention and treatment of PANDAS requires detection and treatment of strep infections with antibiotics. Typically, OCD symptoms worsen with subsequent strep infections, so prompt treatment of strep infections is very important for children with PANDAS-related OCD. OCD symptoms generally improve with antibiotic treatment, but residual OCD symptoms usually remain and can worsen with time, probably because the course of the disorder is influenced by behavioral responses. Thus, treatment beyond antibiotics is often necessary to help the child fully recover.

The Promise of Today

Until recent years, not much could be done for OCD, so children with OCD usually grew into adults with OCD. With our increased ability to understand the disorder, and greater availability of treatments and information, the situation for children with OCD today should be much better. When OCD is recognized early in a child's life, the appropriate treatment can begin before symptoms become ingrained.

Facing the Challenge of OCD

Obsessive-compulsive disorder is scary both for children and for parents. This fear stems in part from not knowing what you're dealing with. As we unmask OCD and expose it for what it is, a treatable neurobehavioral problem, the anxiety and fear will decrease. Arming yourself with knowledge will take the mystery out of this strange journey your family has embarked on. OCD is but one difficulty that your family must face. As with any challenge, you can choose to allow this problem to weaken your family, or you can let it strengthen your family as you work together to expose and conquer the enemy, OCD.

To assist you as you and your child unmask OCD and learn to more effectively deal with it, we've provided *composite* accounts of other families who have faced the same challenge.

Julie, Seven Years Old

Always neat and tidy, Julie felt a need for cleanliness that initially pleased her mother. But as Julie's worries over germs grew, her mother became concerned. The problem began to get out of hand when Julie was in kindergarten. The other children just seemed so nasty to her; runny noses, dirty hands, messy hair—she was sure she'd catch something. Her hands were red and chapped from washing. Now in second grade, she was staying home from school several times a month with vague complaints of headaches and stomachaches.

Tommy, Eight Years Old

Everything had to be in order for Tommy. His books and toys were always arranged perfectly. He got angry when his brothers and sisters disturbed anything and even insisted on cleaning his own room so he could replace everything in its perfect place. Tommy vacuumed and dusted his room daily, for which his brothers teased him. His father tried to talk him out of these silly neatness and cleanliness compulsions. His clothing also had to be perfectly neat. A spot or wrinkle necessitated changing clothes; scuffed shoes were intolerable to Tommy. This brought on family arguments. Both parents thought his behavior was a ploy for new clothes and shoes.

Roberto, Eleven Years Old

Since Roberto had always been a bit of a worrier, his parents thought his latest problems were no different. Unwanted or worrisome thoughts would just seem to pop into his head without warning. Sometimes he would worry that he had said something wrong or hurt someone's feelings. He'd go over past events trying to make sure that all was okay. His parents would reassure him there was nothing to worry about. Other thoughts seemed totally out of place, even to him. Watching TV, he'd get the idea that he might throw the remote control at the TV. To prevent this, he'd make sure another family member was in charge of the remote control. He had similar thoughts about breaking his CD player and stopped using it. Roberto's mother told him to just not listen to the thoughts. He tried, but the thoughts kept coming back and he couldn't help listening to them. Keeping his mind busy seemed to help, so he counted or recited phrases repeatedly. Whatever he tried would help for only a short while and then lose its effectiveness.

Gary, Nine Years Old

Gary was a meticulous student. He often worried about getting every answer right on tests, so much so that he rarely finished them. Halfway through a test, he'd feel compelled to go back and check his answers to previous questions. Then he'd get stuck deliberating about answers he wasn't totally sure of. At home, he would stay up late doing homework, checking his answers over and over. After going to bed he'd get up, turn on the light, check to make sure all his books and papers were in his backpack, then go back to bed. Next he'd get up again to turn off the light. Sometimes the light switch didn't seem to "click" right. He'd switch it on and off, on and off, until it felt right. Gary's mother often came in and found him crying, unable to go back to bed. She'd check his backpack and whatever else he said needed checking and turn out the light. This usually helped and he could finally go to sleep.

Gary's days were filled with similar checking rituals. The kitchen seemed especially dangerous to him. Gary insisted on having all the appliances unplugged when they weren't in use. His mother's compliance with Gary's demands angered his father, who thought his wife was spoiling him and only making things worse.

Rodney, Fourteen Years Old

When Rodney was thirteen years old, the carpets in his family's home were cleaned. For a few hours afterward, he felt a burning sensation in his eyes. The thought that the carpet-cleaning chemicals might have done some permanent damage to his eyes kept bothering him. Over the next few days, he noticed all the chemicals in the house and garage and felt sure they were a danger to the family. His parents weren't convinced of the danger, but they acquiesced. They got rid of insecticides, fertilizers, paints—anything that contained chemicals. Cleaning supplies were next on his list; he insisted that only the mildest could be used. But he couldn't avoid chemicals and cleaning agents completely. The world suddenly seemed like a very dangerous place. When he went outside, he was careful not to walk on lawns because he feared that they might have been recently fertilized. He insisted that family members change their shoes in the garage and put on clean clothes as soon as they got home.

Brenda, Sixteen Years Old

Brenda always tried hard to do the right thing, but she never felt like she was good enough. When she felt that she had done something wrong, discussing it with her parents sometimes helped. They could convince her that the infraction she worried about was minute. She'd often beg for their forgiveness for little things, coming back again and again until she felt okay about a misdeed. Brenda had intrusive thoughts, but she was too embarrassed to tell anyone about them. To rid herself of them she prayed. If she believed her prayers weren't perfect, she'd start over. At first that helped, but as they lost their effectiveness her prayers became more elaborate as she desperately tried to get rid of the thoughts.

Sonya, Twelve Years Old

Sonya came from a family of collectors. Her mother owned more than two thousand dolls and continued to add to her collection. Her father collected anything made of brass. They both saved items that might be useful in the future; for example, they kept twenty old mop and broom handles in the garage because they thought they might come in handy some day. So no one was too concerned when Sonya became a collector herself. When Sonya ran out of space in her room, her mother helped her pack some of her things in boxes to be stored in the garage. But soon her mother became concerned about the difficulty Sonya had parting with things, even to be stored, and was surprised at the variety of things she'd saved. There were school papers, movie tickets, and notes, but also candy wrappers, clothing tags, and some paper items even Sonya couldn't identify.

Your Family's OCD Story

The goals of part 1 of *Helping Your Child with OCD* are to give you information about OCD and the treatment of the disorder, and to help you understand how OCD is affecting the life of your child and your family. On the worksheet that follows, briefly describe your child's OCD symptoms and how they are affecting your family. Before you write down your responses, make copies of the blank worksheet, because you will revisit this exercise later on.

Our Family's Story

My child's chief OCD symptoms: _____

_____

_____

_____

_____

_____

_____

_____

How OCD is affecting my child's life: _____

_____

_____

_____

_____

_____

_____

_____

How OCD is affecting our family's life: _____

_____

_____

_____

_____

_____

_____

_____

Chart 1a

Chapter 2

Unmasking OCD

Children with OCD often live in a world of secrets. People with OCD, children and adults alike, will often hide their symptoms for as long as possible, sometimes for years, even from their families. They know their OCD behaviors are excessive, illogical, or irrational, and that scares them. They often feel both ashamed of their behaviors and afraid that they may be going crazy. Even when children admit that there is a problem, they often minimize the extent of the problem.

When we unmask OCD, we bring the problem out in the open without shame or fear, so it can be correctly diagnosed, understood, and dealt with. This is one of the first steps of recovery. Unmasking OCD helps children to realize that the problem is OCD, not them.

What Is Not OCD

The first step in unmasking your child's symptoms is to discern what is and what is not OCD. Not every thought or behavior that lay people might think are obsessions or compulsions constitute OCD. Some are symptoms of other problems, and some are actually quite "normal."

Childhood Rituals and Avoidance

Rituals and avoidance are normal aspects of a child's development. For example, a three-year-old may insist that the crusts be cut off her sandwiches or that she put her right shoe on before her left. These behaviors provide the child with a sense of security and control over her world. As children develop, they let go of such rigid behaviors and give new ones a try.

Rituals and avoidance behaviors remain common at bedtime, times of separation from parents, and other stressful situations. Most of these behaviors disappear by age eight. However, even older children can engage in ritualistic behaviors as part of normal development, wearing a lucky hat to every ball game; collecting coins, shells, or trinkets; or holding their breath when passing a cemetery for example. These behaviors do not interfere with the child's life. On the contrary, they may even enhance it, because these actions can be fun, aid in learning, or contribute to a sense of mastery or self-control.

OCD behaviors are different from normal behaviors in two major ways. First, the child with OCD believes that the rituals and avoidance are truly necessary to prevent anxiety and possibly danger. Second, OCD behaviors typically disrupt life. For example, think of the game children play that involves avoiding cracks on a school playground or a sidewalk. For most children, accidentally stepping on a crack is no big deal or may even be a funny part of the game. But for a child with OCD, doing so might trigger intense distress ("Maybe Mom is hurt!") and spawn other rituals, even causing him to go home from school to see if his mother is okay.

Superstitions, Religious Rituals, and Prayer

Baseball players kick the ground and touch their caps before they pitch or bat. Actors say "Break a leg" to each other before they go on stage. People routinely "knock on wood." People of many religions pray at particular times every day.

Superstitions and religious rituals can be a normal part of life. The *DSM-IV-TR* states that they suggest OCD only when they are particularly time-consuming or result in significant impairment or distress. It also specifies that ritualistic behavior must exceed cultural norms, or appear inappropriate to others of the same culture or religion, to indicate OCD. For example, if a devout Catholic goes to Mass, says the rosary, and even attends confession daily, this does not necessarily indicate OCD, because the behavior is considered to be within the cultural norm. However, if such a person repeatedly doubted confessing adequately and so returned to confess again, then the behavior would clearly exceed the cultural norm, suggesting OCD.

Many superstitions, religious rituals, and prayers may seem somewhat excessive but are not OCD because they are not driven by uncertainty, anxiety, or distress; do not cause distress or dysfunction; and do not exceed cultural norms. Mental health professionals need to be familiar with a person's culture and motivating thoughts before diagnosing OCD.

Addictions and Addictive Behavior

What if a person craves alcohol, drugs, or nicotine? What about the overwhelming desire to gamble, surf the Internet, or shop? People often confuse these desires with obsessions because the addict seems unable to stop thinking about the substance or activity until the desire has been satisfied. To the addict, it feels like he or she is "obsessed" with the desire and "compelled" to act on the impulse.

The difference is that addictions develop because of a positive reinforcement cycle rather than a negative one. The behaviors originally start and are repeated because the individual finds them pleasurable, rather than because the behaviors relieve a bad feeling, as is the case with OCD. However, with overuse, the addictive substance or activity stops providing the same amount of pleasure, and so the behaviors are intensified or increased.

With chemical addictions, the process can go even further. The user's brain chemistry changes so that without the drug the individual feels anxious or stressed. Over time, the user needs the drug in order to simply feel normal. Thus, a behavior that originally brought pleasure (positive reinforcement) becomes necessary to relieve chronic discomfort (negative reinforcement). It now continues both because it alleviates discomfort and because it provides pleasure.

Nervous Habits

Like OCD rituals, habits like thumb sucking, skin picking, nail biting, and hair pulling tend to increase when the individual feels anxiety or stress, and are engaged in to relieve that stress. Nervous habits can become so ingrained, like OCD behaviors, that they seem ritualistic, become almost automatic, and are difficult to stop. But these kinds of habits are actually impulse-control problems.

Like addictions, these behaviors are begun because they feel pleasurable or satisfying to the individual (positive reinforcement). These habits are not meaningful in the way compulsions are in OCD; they are not purposeful acts intended to relieve anxiety associated with specific thoughts and feelings (obsessions). However, as is the case with OCD, it turns out that some people may be a bit more neurologically prone to developing nervous habits, especially trichotillomania (hair pulling). Because of this neurological vulnerability, trichotillomania is considered by many to be a cousin of OCD.

Cutting and Self-Mutilation

Like people with impulse-control problems, those who engage in more serious self-injury, such as cutting and self-mutilation, often report that they do so automatically, without realizing what they are doing, and that they "can't stop." They sometimes report strong urges to engage in the behavior, typically when they feel upset.

These are highly complex behaviors that do not automatically or neatly fall into any one diagnostic category. For some, the behavior may be part of an addiction-like cycle driven by positive reinforcement, with the person originally having enjoyed some sensory aspect of the experience or sense of control rendered by the behavior. For others, it is more clearly a self-soothing behavior, with the person using it to modulate negative emotions such as sadness, emptiness, and depression. For many, it is associated with the experience of dissociation, or "zoning out." Cutting and self-mutilation are very rarely compulsions as they occur in OCD: they are rarely spurred by uncertainty or intended to preserve a sense of safety. However, these behaviors should be taken very seriously, because serious physical harm can easily result.

Tics (and Tourette's Syndrome)

Tics are another problem considered by many to be related to OCD because tics are caused by neurological factors and they are often associated with OCD. Tics are movements, gestures, vocal sounds (such as throat clearing and verbal phrases), and even sniffing actions that a person feels "compelled" to perform. Tourette's syndrome is diagnosed when there are multiple tics, specifically when at least two motor tics and one vocal tic are present.

Tics are different from OCD rituals or compulsions in a number of ways. First, they are predominantly involuntary. Once the itch to tic arises, it usually continues to build until the person gives in. Eventually, the person *must* tic. He or she can only control whether to postpone the tic or not. (Many people with tics report "saving up" their tics until they have a private moment when they tic freely, "getting it out of their system.") In contrast, people with OCD actually have the capacity to abstain from their rituals.

Second, with tics, the urge builds until it is satisfied. With OCD, the urge to ritualize, or engage in compulsions, gradually goes away and the anxiety subsides when the urge is resisted for a long enough period.

Third, tics do not appear to be related to any kind of reinforcement; they are neither pleasure driven (as in addictions and habits) nor relief driven (as in OCD). As a result, for the most part, the frequency of the tic does not change as a result of changes in reinforcement properties over time. (Compulsions lose their power to remove distress; addictions lose the power to provide pleasure; both result in intensifying behavior frequency.) An exception to this is that many children with tics also have OCD, and sometimes their compulsion is the same as their tic behavior. For such a child, sometimes the "tic" *is* a compulsion, done purposefully in response to an obsession. At other times, the tic is *just* a tic. And sometimes, the tic is really a little bit of both.

Eating Disorders

People with eating disorders such as anorexia nervosa, bulimia, and compulsive eating usually appear "obsessed" with food or their weight. Just like people with OCD, addictions, and nervous habits, they engage in repetitive behaviors (e.g., counting calories, binging, and purging). The causes of eating disorders vary. Some people with eating disorders clearly suffer from an addictive type of process; their repetitive behaviors bring pleasure, often in the form of weight loss. Some suffer from a relief-driven process (like OCD), their repetitive behaviors relieving feelings of being fat, ugly, or disgusting.

There are people with OCD whose rituals and avoidance practices involve food and result in extreme weight loss or weight gain; their purpose is to respond to an obsession (such as fear of poison, vomiting, or "getting fat") and reduce anxiety or danger. It is not uncommon for such individuals to be misdiagnosed with an eating disorder.

Body Dysmorphic Disorder

People with body dysmorphic disorder (BDD) have intrusive, upsetting thoughts about some aspect of their appearance that they think is ugly. Usually, the flaw is minor, hardly noticeable, and certainly not important to others. Often these individuals avoid social situations because they do not want others to see their flaw. Sometimes they attempt to minimize their flaw, with efforts ranging from wearing makeup to spending their life's savings on plastic surgery. Many repeatedly check their flaw to see whether it shows or has worsened. Unlike people with OCD, the individual with BDD is not likely to recognize that the concern is irrational. And, with BDD, the "obsession" is limited to a specific upsetting concern, which does not change over time. Despite these differences, the disorders are so similar that the treatments for both are similar.

Worry and Generalized Anxiety

Some children, just like some adults, seem to be natural worriers. They constantly worry about what's going to happen tomorrow, what happened yesterday, and what may happen in twenty years. You may wonder if these are obsessions.

Well, kind of. These children closely resemble those with *purely obsessional* OCD. Purely obsessional OCD (actually a misnomer) is a form of OCD in which compulsions are predominantly unobservable mental activities. Worriers and pure obsessionals both mentally review or dwell on past situations or interactions seeking certainty; repeatedly ask questions seeking reassurance; or excessively plan, problem solve, or engage in other mental behaviors to ensure desired outcomes. The differences between pure obsessionals and worriers are minor. One difference is that the concerns of a worrier are more fluid—there is usually a "worry of the week (or day or hour)." Another difference is that worries usually seem more ordinary, plausible, or likely than the obsessions of a person with purely obsessional OCD. A worrier may fret about an upcoming test, a conversation at school, or Nana's health. A child with purely obsessional OCD may worry about any typical OCD concern, such as harm, illness, contamination, bad luck, disaster, or violent thoughts. However, the concerns will remain more fixed than those of a general worrier and the specific concerns will be more implausible, "Maybe Mom (who is in good health) will die," for example. As with a general worrier, the child's neutralizing or safety behaviors are predominantly mental activities. Many of the same treatment strategies are effective for both pure obsessionals and worriers.

Specific Phobias

Some children have extreme fears of specific things, like thunderstorms, dogs, vomiting, and so on. Children with these problems engage in avoidance of their feared object or situation just as children with OCD do. For these children, avoidance strengthens and maintains the fear much as it does in children with OCD. The main difference between children with specific phobias and children with OCD is that the majority of children (and adults) who have OCD engage in compulsions while those with specific phobias do not.

Panic Disorder

The experience of having a panic attack is common for anyone with any anxiety disorder. It can occur in people who do not have an anxiety problem. A panic attack is an unpleasant experience that occurs at times of high physiological arousal, generally when a person is highly stressed or frightened. It is the body's alarm reaction; the symptoms are essentially the harmless side effects of the body's preparation for fight or flight. Symptoms of a panic attack include racing heart, difficulty breathing, chest pain, dizziness, feelings of unreality, choking sensations, nausea, abdominal distress, tingling sensations, fear of going crazy, and fear of loss of control. For a panic attack to be diagnosed, at least four symptoms must be noted and the experience must peak in a very short period of time.

Panic disorder occurs only when a person has experienced panic attacks and has developed a fear of the panic attacks. Thus, since panic attacks are common in any anxiety disorder there are many people who suffer from panic disorder in addition to another anxiety problem. So some children with OCD can also develop panic disorder in addition to their OCD. But the experience of panic attacks does not necessarily indicate OCD, nor does having OCD necessarily lead to the development of panic disorder.

Depression and Suicidal Thoughts

Some people report having recurrent thoughts of killing themselves. Are these obsessions? The short answer is that they may or may not be. Distinguishing between depression and OCD can be difficult because both disorders can involve mental rumination, and both can include the experience of feeling anxious. Furthermore, people with severe OCD often are depressed. So, what is OCD and what is depression?

When people are depressed, their thinking often gets stuck on the subjects of their own worthlessness and being better off dead. Their difficulty dismissing these thoughts and moving on to others (such as uplifting thoughts) is similar to the difficulty OCD sufferers have letting go of their intrusive obsessions. But unlike someone with OCD, the seriously depressed person generally accepts and believes all of his or her negative thoughts fully and may not react to such thoughts with alarm. He or she rarely thinks, "Maybe I'm going crazy; this thought is extreme!" In fact, thoughts of dying may be an escape fantasy for a depressed person, bringing a feeling of relief or longing. When people with OCD have obsessions about harming themselves, the thoughts tend to fill them with dread and anxiety.

Obsessive-Compulsive Personality Disorder (OCPD)

People with OCPD are perfectionists preoccupied with details, rules, lists, and order-liness. They are inflexible and feel that they always need to be in control. They are not distressed by the overbearing rules and requirements they impose on themselves and others (although those around them may indeed feel disturbed). In contrast, people with OCD are greatly distressed by the requirements they feel they must follow. Personality disorders are usually not diagnosed until adulthood, but such patterns can sometimes be seen in children. However, perfectionist traits that do not interfere with everyday life do not usually develop into OCPD.

The Flavors of OCD

Now that you have an idea of what is *not* OCD, it's time to discuss what OCD *is*. Many OCD symptoms are obvious, but others are quite subtle and often go unrecognized. They can masquerade as ordinary daily activities. For example, our culture encourages hand washing before meals, so family members may not notice that one child's washing is too thorough. Additionally, symptoms are not necessarily static; they can expand and shift. A child who washes his hands excessively might develop a concern about electrical outlets.

We hope that understanding the types of OCD will help you and your child detect OCD symptoms early, before they become entrenched. We have organized this section by the categories of compulsions, addressing within each category the obsessions that generally drive and motivate them. Understanding the logical connections between compulsions and obsessions will aid you in recognizing symptoms when they emerge.

While reading this section, keep in mind that some people with OCD have just one type of compulsion, while many have more than one kind. When individuals have multiple concerns and compulsive behaviors, a general theme often runs through them. The themes of obsessions tend to relate to the values or things that the person holds most dear. For example, a young child who has longed for a new sibling may be horrified by sudden obsessions about hitting or hurting the baby. Adolescents embarking on dating can have obsessive doubts about their sexual orientation. A pious child may struggle with the thought that maybe he really wants to worship Satan. A gentle and responsible child can be tormented by thoughts that her carelessness will kill her family. *Anything* can become an obsession if it represents a threat that is personally relevant.

You may also notice as you read the descriptions below that you yourself fit into at least one of the categories. Most people do. When people engage in these behaviors to a reasonable degree, the behaviors tend to help their functioning. In people with OCD, the behaviors seem to develop a life of their own and interfere with daily functioning.

Checking (and Reassurance Seeking)

Checking means repeatedly confirming something, such as making sure a light is off, a door is locked, or one's clothes are clean. The obsessions that motivate the checking are sometimes irrational fears of harm resulting from some sort of error. Or they may be related to concerns over imperfection, asymmetry, or incompleteness. Examples include making sure that all of one's Os are properly closed in a handwritten essay, that all pencils are lined up in a row, and that all of the dirt was vacuumed off the floor. Often, checking is related logically to the obsessions, but it can be loosely related. For example, a child who has had an obsession about harm coming to her baby brother might feel the need to call home to check on her baby brother, to be sure that counting to five while climbing her school steps worked to protect him. An interesting observation is that almost every obsession has some checking related to it.

Repeatedly seeking reassurance is really a verbal form of checking. An individual will ask questions or make statements intended to get a response that will alleviate uncertainty, such as "You said the homework was problems 3 though 21?" or "These obsessions will go away?" Often the questions will be repeated in the same way each time: "Are you sure?" "Are you sure?" Sometimes they will be changed, but their intent remains the same: "You don't think I'm sick?" "So, I'm okay then?" One clue that such questions are excessive is that usually one question is insufficient. The child may even feel that it is necessary to elicit the same answer a certain number of times. However, keep in mind that repetitive questioning in young children is normal. For young children, repeating a question aids mastery and learning. For children with OCD, the questioning interferes with functioning.

Washing and Cleaning of Self or Objects

People with OCD may feel a need to wash excessively, wash in a particular way or a certain number of times, or even wash with bleach, to ensure thorough cleanliness. Related obsessions are usually about contamination by germs, body fluids, dirt, chemicals, or other foreign substances. Washing can even be related to maintaining perfection. Or washing may simply alleviate unwanted feelings of stickiness, grime, or general yuckiness. Children with contamination concerns often demand that family members follow cleaning rituals.

Ordering

Ordering, or placing things in order, is an effort to relieve anxiety or combat anxious thoughts by arranging certain items in particular ways. Children with this kind of compulsion may get upset if their toys or books are out of place. They may even insist that furniture in the rest of the house be arranged in a certain way. Their demands for order usually continue to increase. They may also have a need for symmetry, to have certain things even. Fears driving these behaviors can range from harm (the behaviors "magically" prevent a specific or vague disaster) to something not feeling "just right."

Repeating, Touching, or Tapping

Some people are compelled to redo certain actions (such as walking through a door) or touch or tap certain things (such as door frames). Often, the repeating, touching, or tapping serves to "clear" or prevent a bad thought or feeling, ensuring only good thoughts or feelings. Sometimes, the person believes that these behaviors will prevent the bad thought from occurring. For some people, the repeating is not necessarily tied to certain actions or objects; rather, they repeat whatever they were doing when an obsession or "not right" feeling came upon them. This can be quite confusing to observers because the behaviors appear (and often are) random.

Mental Rituals and "Pure Obsessionals"

Mental rituals are purposeful, voluntary thoughts intended to reassure, achieve certainty, protect from harm, or reduce anxiety. Examples include counting; thinking special words, phrases, or prayers; thinking or imagining the opposite of the obsession; mental reviewing (replaying of events or conversations); mental debating (endless arguing over some issue, moral point, decision, or question); and wishing (fantasizing about how life should be different than it is). An example of wishing would be to respond to a thought about death by fantasizing about a world without death and being caught up in the idea that people should not die. Wishing is a mental ritual brought to our attention by Jon Grayson, Ph.D. It's not a compulsion that has been routinely recognized by OCD therapists, but it's one that seems to make a lot of sense to us. These ritualized mental compulsions are different from mulling something over or rumination because they are efforts to get certainty and neutralize anxiety (Grayson 2003).

Some of these compulsions are more ritualized than others. For example, counting to a particular number and thinking an exact phrase are highly ritualized because there is extreme rigidity to the content of the thought. Mental reviewing, mental debating, and wishing are hardly ritualized at all and more closely resemble mulling something over.

Mental compulsions can occur in response to *any* obsession. However, they are most often connected with unacceptable sexual, aggressive, or blasphemous thoughts; neutral obsessions; and unacceptable ideas or facts. Unacceptable sexual, aggressive, or blasphemous thoughts often trigger recitation of magical phrases, counting, thinking the opposite, or compulsive praying. Neutral obsessions—thoughts and images that are not alarming in themselves but are distressing because they will not go away—frequently trigger wishing that the thought would go away. Finally, unacceptable ideas or facts also trigger wishing, mental debating, and reassurance seeking.

It used to be thought that pure obsessionals did not have compulsions and were treatment resistant. Experts now recognize that pure obsessionals have primarily mental compulsions and respond to treatment as do people with other forms of OCD. However, treatment can be trickier because their compulsions are often mistaken for obsessions by both patient and therapist.

Scrupulosity

People with scrupulosity focus excessively on religious, moral, or ethical issues. Some pray or confess constantly or take religious rituals to an extreme. Obsessions driving this behavior can include doubts as to whether they are fulfilling their obligations correctly, fears of damnation or God's wrath, or worries about blasphemous thoughts. Some people with scrupulosity engage in endless information gathering, debating, and reassurance seeking in order to relieve some doubt regarding a religious, moral, or ethical dilemma. These activities can spiral endlessly in their own minds or spill over to others (priests, rabbis, or family members). Overall, people with scrupulosity do not derive peace and contentment from their activities. Rather, their religious and moral practices interfere with healthy functioning.

Hoarding

Hoarding is the act or practice of accumulating very large amounts of stuff. Some people's hoard grows from excessive collecting. People with this type of OCD see value in what others consider trash or junk. For many, the hoard results from avoiding making the decisions involved in sorting through and tossing out items. Often, they cannot stand the risk of making a mistake and being without something they might want later. Frequently, people with large collections suffer from tendencies toward both excessive gathering and avoiding throwing things away.

Many other people who hoard, especially children, fear letting go of their stuff. Some report feeling that the saved objects have their own life forces and sensibilities. Still others say that the items have somehow become or contain a part of themselves or their own history. For these people, discarding items feels tantamount to killing something, being disrespectful of someone, or cutting out and discarding a chunk of their own soul.

Changing and Evolving Symptoms

Because the feeling of certainty is endlessly elusive, compulsions tend to become progressively more complex and time-consuming. When one check or washing fails to bring the desired and expected relief, the apparent solution is to do more. Sometimes, "more" means an apparently unrelated action that becomes associated with the existing ritual simply because it happened to occur just when relief arrived. For example, a child might report, "Flexing my toes three times didn't work like usual; but when I blinked at the same time, it felt right." Now, the ritual includes flexing toes *and* blinking.

Occasionally, logic dictates extending rituals to other situations. If hands need washing in one circumstance then it stands to reason they should also be washed in another comparable circumstance. For example, if someone has obsessions about anthrax after touching the mail that result in hand washing, then it is likely the same person will find it important to wash surfaces that the mail has touched. Additionally, a change in routine that brings accompanying stress can often bring to the fore new obsessive concerns or intensify existing concerns and behaviors. Furthermore, one set of fears sometimes subsides only to be replaced by another.

At this point, you should have both a basic understanding of OCD and an appreciation of some of the "flavors" of OCD. All of this knowledge will help you unmask your child's symptoms. However, correctly diagnosing and assessing OCD is complicated. Do have your child evaluated by a qualified mental health provider if you suspect OCD. If your child is not diagnosed correctly and does not receive the right treatment, his or her problems can worsen.

One thing that you and only you, as a parent, can do to help your child is to gain some understanding of what it *feels* like to have OCD. Then you'll be better equipped to observe your child and your family to determine how much and in what ways OCD is affecting them. In chapter 3, we'll address the impact of OCD on both your child and your family, and what can happen if these problems are not addressed.

Identifying Your Child's Obsessions and Compulsions

In part 2, you will systematically observe how OCD affects your child and family. For now, list below the compulsions your child performs and the obsessions that appear to be behind them. Make copies of the blank worksheet first, because you will revisit this exercise later.

OCD Symptoms

Compulsions	Obsessions behind the Compulsions

Chart 2a

Chapter 3

The Impact of OCD

Assessing the impact of OCD on your child and your family is important for many reasons. Having some understanding of what your child *feels* is essential for you to fully empathize with and adequately support your child. Not knowing the influence of OCD on your child's behavior might lead you to incorrectly attribute other difficulties you observe to personality flaws. Without understanding how devastating this disorder can be, you might underestimate the need to get your child the right help or make changes yourself. Finally, unless you appreciate the impact of OCD on your family's functioning, OCD can trick you and other family members into helping it ruin your child's life.

What Does an OCD Moment Feel Like?

The discussion below is credited to Jon Grayson, Ph.D., and is adapted from his presentations on OCD. To understand your child's extreme distress when he or she is assaulted by an obsession and is gripped by fear and uncertainty, consider a comparable experience in your own life. Imagine that your child has recently gotten her driver's license. She is responsible and always lets you know where and with whom she's going, and when she expects to return home. She asks for permission to take her friends to a movie on Friday night. Her driving skills are good, and she's driven at night, so you agree. But when the night arrives, the weather is cold and rainy. It might snow. You want to tell your child that she will need to reschedule. But your spouse accuses you of being a worrywart and persuades you to let her go as planned.

Now it's midnight, and it's snowing. She was due back more than an hour ago. You've heard nothing. You can't sleep. You can't watch television. You can't read. You can't do anything except think about what might have happened. You imagine your car crashed into a telephone pole, with your child lying beside it. You are on the verge of tears. You are so angry that you can't look at your spouse without wanting to scream. You feel helpless and terrified. You are saying prayers. You want to call the hospitals and the police.

On some level, you know that she is probably safe, that you're jumping to horrific conclusions. You know that there are an infinite number of possible reasons to explain why she has not called or returned home. But every time you try to convince yourself, another "what if?" thought emerges. You just cannot trust that your child is safe until you know for sure. So you continue to worry and watch the clock until she walks through the door.

This feeling of intense worry that defies logic is what people with OCD feel during an OCD moment when an obsession takes hold. The majority of people with OCD can recognize, most of the time, that their worries and fears are probably senseless. But in the midst of an OCD moment, when the person is caught in the cycle of fear and uncertainty, the doubt intensifies. He or she thinks, "Maybe my worries really are justified. Maybe the elaborate ritual is necessary. Do I really want to take the risk?" The need for certainty takes over because the distress is so extreme. For the child with OCD, there are no consistent assumptions of safety when OCD is talking. Intense worry *feels* like what your child feels in an OCD moment. And for a child with OCD, those moments occur many times a day.

Still, the scenario described above does not quite capture the whole experience of an OCD moment. What is missing is the sense of embarrassment, helplessness, and loss of control that also accompanies the moment. Because, even while gripped by extreme fear, children with OCD know that what they are doing and feeling is "weird." So, they feel even more out of control and "crazy." It's a double punch: the obsession terrorizes, and the lack of control terrorizes even more.

What Does It Feel Like to Live with OCD Every Day?

The answer to this largely depends on whether the problem has been diagnosed, whether the child knows about and understands the disorder, and where the child is in the process of recovery. As we mentioned above, OCD moments come with a large dose of embarrassment, shame, and fear of being crazy. When the disorder is undiagnosed and worsening, this embarrassment and shame can become pervasive, seriously eroding self-esteem and self-confidence. Beyond that, the chronic anxiety and frantic OCD activity consume the child's life, often leading to depression.

The situation changes once a child is diagnosed and educated about OCD. Diagnosis and education alleviate the fear of going crazy—both because the problem is named and because the child learns that crazy people don't usually worry about going crazy. Lingering concerns about being defective are generally dispelled when the child learns that OCD is probably just a downside to his or her many positive qualities. Most people with OCD tend to be extremely intelligent, imaginative, moral, thoughtful, and creative. After successfully meeting the challenge of recovery, people with OCD often view the disorder as an asset. Their personal struggle gives them a sense of empathy for others, while the strength and perseverance they found within themselves become a point of personal pride.

The Impact of OCD on Development

The impact of unmanaged OCD can be devastating to a child's academic development. Although many children with OCD are quite intelligent, doing schoolwork can trigger specific obsessions and rituals that make completing academic tasks nearly impossible. The anxiety of OCD can also spawn difficulties with concentration, causing academic achievement to plummet. Students who have received A's "without lifting a pencil" suddenly begin to fail.

Many students in this situation stop thinking of themselves as smart, bright, or talented. Their sense of competence takes a hard hit and often their love of school and learning evaporates. It's not difficult to see how this drop in self-confidence could interfere with a child's future. Many adult OCD patients report that they struggled in school and did not pursue a career or educational goal because they felt unable to manage the work.

OCD can be a devastating influence on a child's social development as well. Many children with OCD are very social and care deeply about other people. Yet, when their OCD takes over, they become isolated, in part because of the shame and embarrassment they feel. Shame can motivate a child to withdraw so that others won't know about the problem. Also, the more time-consuming and demanding OCD becomes, the less time or attention is available to the affected child for normal childhood activities. Such children may feel that they can't play outside with friends, because their bathroom will be too far away (they feel reluctant to venture into unknown bathrooms where germs may be rampant or they want the privacy of their own bathroom so they can wash sufficiently without risk of being observed), or because they need that time to make sure their homework has no mistakes or their belongings are correctly organized. For other children, withdrawal has to do with avoiding situations that might trigger obsessions.

Whatever the reasons, such withdrawal from social situations can be damaging to a child's development. Activity (physical, social, and productive) is necessary for the development of talents, likes and dislikes, and a sense of competence. Also, social interaction is necessary for a child to master age-appropriate social skills. Withdrawal is also often accompanied by overreliance on family, which interferes with the development of autonomy. Such overreliance can also reduce a child's self-confidence or engender an inflated sense of entitlement that interferes with making and keeping friends.

How Bad Can It Get?

We have all heard of adults who live like prisoners in one room of their parents' home because their obsessions and compulsions have robbed them of their ability to function. This is indeed a possible outcome, and keeping this in mind can help your family and your child stay focused on helping him or her get better. However, do remember that this is only one of many possible futures, and being trapped by OCD does not have to be in your child's future. Treatments available today can reduce symptoms by 50 to 80 percent. Thus, a productive life, with OCD only running in the background, is within your child's grasp.

Many parents want to know what will happen if their child goes without treatment. Unfortunately, very little research on this issue has been done. It is possible that some children will outgrow the symptoms. Additionally, because OCD symptoms wax and wane, it's possible that your child will have periods during which they struggle with their symptoms and also experience periods where they are relatively symptom free. What we do know is that many adults with OCD report an onset in childhood with a gradually worsening course until they received treatment. These adults say that they wish their problem had been identified and addressed sooner. By getting your child help, educating yourself, and learning what you can do, you are working to save your child from ever needing to make that wish.

Identifying OCD Symptoms

Besides revealing the obsessions and compulsions of OCD, unmasking OCD also involves looking for other signs of OCD that are having a major impact on a child's life. Making note of them will help with diagnosis and will help you identify what problems need work. Indicate symptoms that are having an impact on your child's life by checking the box.

- ☐ unusual secretiveness about activities and behaviors, and what they are doing with their time

- ☐ poor performance in school; daydreaming and inattention, falling grades, difficulty taking tests and completing homework

- ☐ reluctance to participate in extracurricular activities or family functions

- ☐ refusal to participate in (or fear of) new situations or activities

- ☐ refusal to participate in (or fear of) activities once enjoyed, for no apparent reason

- ☐ withdrawal from friends

- ☐ questions, worrying, or pleas for reassurance

☐ excessive need to control the environment and the behavior of others; getting very upset when losing control

☐ excessive fear of harm coming to self or others

☐ extreme perfectionism, indecision, or slowness

☐ rumination about details; going over past events

☐ excessive need for certainty

☐ hair pulling, nail biting, excessive grooming, tics, or twitches

OCD's Impact on the Family

The symptoms of OCD influence every part of a child's life, eventually spilling over to the family. It's not just the child but also the family members who end up suffering considerable distress.

What Does It Feel Like to Have OCD in the Family?

Parents sometimes say that having OCD in their family is like having an intruder take up residence in their home and call all the shots. Parents often feel helpless, not knowing what to do or whom to turn to for help. They also feel guilty, like they have somehow failed—their child is struggling, and the parents don't know what to do or say. Frequently, they are angry at their child, wanting to scream, "Stop it already!" At other times, their anger may be directed at God or the world. Parents often feel out of control themselves, and they may even feel at fault for being angry, frustrated, and stressed.

Similarly, life for the siblings of a child with OCD is no picnic. When the disorder arises, the house no longer feels like their home. Predictability and routine fly out the window; shouting, crying, and power struggles may erupt at a moment's notice. The unaffected siblings are told to "be strong," "be understanding," or "take the high road," but they often struggle with anger and resentment, feeling ignored or forgotten because of their sibling's OCD.

In some cases a sibling or parent is a key part of the child's OCD symptoms, for example, when the obsession centers on contamination from the sibling or parent. These cases trigger complex emotional reactions from the object of the obsession, with that person thinking, "Does he not love me anymore?" or "How dare she say I am disgusting and dirty?" or "Am I really as dirty or disgusting as my child (or sibling) seems to believe?" Another example is a child's obsession that one parent might die. Being the focus of such intense concern nearly always causes that parent to feel guilty, wondering "Have I done something to cause this?" As a result, the parent feels an even stronger pull to carry this burden for the child and assure him or her that everything is fine.

How Does OCD Affect Family Functioning?

Whether or not you realize it, your family has probably been tricked into joining in and supporting the OCD. In attempting to help a child function and maintain a "normal" life, families often adopt avoidant strategies and sometimes even aid children in their rituals. For example, you may have found yourself standing outside the shower in a designated spot holding a fresh, clean towel and your daughter's clean clothes so that when she emerges from the shower she can dry and dress herself without worrying that her towel or clothes have touched something disgusting. Similarly, you may have stockpiled soap, shampoo, clothes, linens, or other materials so that when an obsession hits and something that seems perfectly good is somehow "ruined," you have more supplies on hand so that a meltdown can be avoided. You may be organizing and checking your child's book bag before school according to his rigid rules, just so he can catch his bus and get to school on time. Family members behave like this so OCD will cause less distress and occupy less of the child's time and because, like the child, they see no other way out. The parents' goal is to contain the problem until it passes or the child can get control.

At first, these strategies may seem to succeed. However, OCD is insidious, and these efforts gradually create more problems. The benefits of safety behaviors are just as temporary when the family does them as when the child does them, and the behaviors strengthen OCD's hold on the child just as effectively. So the effects of the behaviors fade, and the OCD takes over more and more of the family's life.

When this happens, parents no longer seem available to their other children because they are so involved with the sibling with OCD. Family rules and expectations no longer seem fair; the siblings are still expected to follow them, but the child with OCD is not. Saying what they want is also no longer okay, because it might set off a reaction in the child with OCD. As a result, conflicts between siblings may increase markedly. Some siblings may respond by emotionally disconnecting, spending as little time at home as possible. When they are home, they seem separate and distant. Other siblings notice that the neediest child gets the attention in the family and hence develop a severe problem of their own.

Often, family members are just as embarrassed by the OCD and related family problems as the child is and are just as eager to keep the problem hidden from the rest of the world. And even if they are not ashamed themselves, they often respect their child's wishes for secrecy. But the urge to hide problems frequently works to isolate the entire family. Parents may bow out of family gatherings and may pull away from good friends lest they notice that something is wrong. Siblings may stop having friends over to spend the night. Self-imposed isolation leaves many families with little support and makes them more vulnerable to the OCD.

The stress on the family can also lead to marital discord. Spouses may not agree on how to handle the crisis or may be angry because the burden is not equally shared. Sometimes spouses even blame each other for the development of the problem in the first place.

Finally, the impact on the family can extend to the economic realm. Sometimes parents miss work because of their child's OCD crises. In extreme cases, absenteeism can lead to job loss. Or a parent may decide to stop working in order to be more available to the child. The cost of treatment, both medication and therapy, can drain financial resources further.

We apologize if you have felt distressed while reading this chapter. We have not elaborated on the possible impacts of OCD in order to depress you—we have done so in order to communicate to you that if your child (or family) is struggling in the ways that we have described *you are not alone,* and *it is not your fault.* Rather, all of the potential effects that we have described are the understandable consequences of a family member having a serious disorder. Let this information motivate you to get treatment for your child and to make changes within your family that will support your child's recovery. Before going on to the next chapter, review the information you've learned in this chapter and fill out new copies of the Our Family's Story and OCD Symptoms worksheets from chapters 1 and 2.

Part II

Selecting Treatment and Seeking Help

In reading this book you've taken a major step toward helping your child cope with OCD. The first step in helping your child is gaining more understanding of the problem. You now understand that this is a no-fault disorder and that a primary neurological component and a subsequent learned component form the basis of the disorder. You're beginning to recognize the symptoms despite the numerous disguises OCD can assume. You've learned that an intolerance of uncertainty is fundamental to all obsessive-compulsive symptoms. Finally, you've learned that OCD can wreak havoc in the life of your child and your family. You appreciate now, if you didn't before, that OCD can be a formidable enemy that must be stopped.

Now you need to learn how OCD can be overcome. In part 2, we will educate you regarding treatment options, and we will help you to analyze these options so that you can make a decision about treatment. We will walk you through the process of finding experts.

OCD is scary for children and parents. This fear stems partly from not knowing what to do and what to expect. Arming yourself with knowledge about treatment will take the mystery out of this strange journey. Through all of this, keep in mind and help your child understand that OCD is but one difficulty that any family can face. As with any challenge, you can choose to allow this challenge to weaken or strengthen your family as you work together to conquer the enemy, OCD.

Chapter 4

Effective Treatments for OCD

Years ago, the treatment options for people with OCD were quite limited and generally ineffective. During the past few decades, this situation has improved. Research has led to the development of highly effective treatments. So, although you and your child may feel very unlucky to have this problem, we believe that you and your child are fortunate. Your child now has a much better chance than ever before of being successfully treated and going on to lead a productive and fulfilling life.

Effective treatments are available in the form of medication and cognitive behavioral therapy. About 75 percent of individuals have some response to appropriate treatment (Yaryura-Tobias and Neziroglu 1997). Individuals differ considerably in their response to treatment. For some, treatment seems to wipe out the problem. For others it may have little or no effect. But for the majority, it makes OCD noticeably easier to manage. Unfortunately, as yet, we cannot routinely predict who will respond best to which treatments, and so the choice of treatment often comes down to personal preferences, professional guidelines, and availability.

Choosing a Treatment Strategy

Choosing how to proceed can be quite difficult for parents. Psychotherapy or medication or both? What kind of medication? What kind of therapy? When to start treatment? The decision-making process can feel overwhelming. In order to help you make these decisions, we'll examine the choices, including the advantages and disadvantages of each.

Option 1: Medication Therapy (SSRIs and SRIs)

For many OCD patients, medication works, and for some it works quite well. The effect most people report is a weakening or lessening of the obsessive thoughts and urges to ritualize. People seem to feel that the whole experience is made less intense. The classes of drugs that have been found most useful in the treatment of OCD are antidepressants that boost the activity of a neurotransmitter in the brain called *serotonin*. These drugs are referred to as *serotonin reuptake inhibitors* (SRIs) and *selective serotonin reuptake inhibitors* (SSRIs). The difference between the two types has to do with how specific their action is to certain neurotransmitters. SSRIs target only serotonin, while SRIs also affect other neurotransmitters in the brain. SSRIs and SRIs used to treat OCD include clomipramine (Anafranil), fluoxetine (Prozac), fluvoxamine (Luvox), paroxetine (Paxil), sertraline (Zoloft), citalopram (Celexa), venlafaxine (Effexor), and the newest on the market, escitalopram oxalate (Lexopro). The advantages of these medications include the following:

◊ The medications are readily available; all you need is a doctor (preferably a psychiatrist) and a pharmacy.

◊ Using them is practically effortless; all you have to *do* is take them as prescribed.

◊ They are also used to treat other anxiety disorders and depression, which often accompany OCD.

There are disadvantages, however, to weigh against these strong benefits:

◊ These medications have physiological side effects that some patients cannot or will not tolerate. Most, such as restlessness and sleepiness, are mild and temporary and are only bothersome during the first few weeks of treatment. Others, such as excessive weight gain and heartburn, are more troublesome. Some of these side effects may necessitate taking additional medications. In rare cases, more serious side effects such as seizures can develop, requiring discontinuation of the medication.

◊ Unfortunately, the FDA has so far approved only four of these medications specifically for treatment of OCD in children, and none for children under age six: Anafranil (age ten and up), Luvox (age eight and up), Zoloft (age six and up), and Prozac (age seven and up). Clinical trials needed for FDA approval are

expensive and are much less frequently conducted on children than adults. Therefore, most of what we know about these medications is based on the results of
clinical trials with adults. Many doctors will assume that the drugs will have similar
effects on children as on adults and will prescribe for children drugs that have
been found effective for adults despite the absence of official FDA approval. This
common practice is referred to as "off-label" prescribing.

◊ Unknown long-term effects may be associated with these drugs. Because SRIs and
SSRIs are relatively new drug types, no studies have examined these drugs over
periods of years. We have no reason to expect long-term ill effects, but we cannot
make any claims that these drugs are risk free.

◊ If a patient stops taking one of these medications, the symptoms are likely to
return.

◊ Taking a medication sometimes causes people to feel embarrassed or even
defective, like helpless victims of their biology. They may suffer poor self-esteem
and lower self-confidence. As a consequence, they may be less likely to make
choices that could contribute to their recovery.

◊ These medications can be expensive. Sometimes the costs will be covered by
insurance benefits and sometimes they will not. And since symptoms may
reemerge if the patient discontinues the drug, someone with OCD will usually
continue taking the drug indefinitely. The expense can add up to quite a large sum
over a lifetime.

◊ Finally, for some OCD patients, medication just does not seem to help enough.
For these patients, trying to find the "right" medication can be frustrating and
demoralizing and can constitute a waste of money and time.

Option 2: Psychotherapy (Cognitive Behavioral Therapy)

For many people with OCD, a particular type of psychotherapy, cognitive behavioral
therapy (CBT), works. Similar to the medication treatment described above, for some it
works quite well. You may wonder why any psychotherapy would be beneficial in a
disorder that has strong biological underpinnings. Many people would assume that a brain
glitch would require drugs or surgery to treat or repair. However, the brain is not a static
mechanism like a personal computer. Rather, it actually changes and modifies both its
"software" and even some of its "hardware" based on its activity. Dr. Jeffrey Schwartz
(1996), author of *Brain Lock: Free Yourself from Obsessive-Compulsive Disorder,* and Dr. Lewis
Baxter demonstrated through positron emission tomography (PET) scan studies that brain
areas that were overactive in people with OCD before treatment changed and became
comparable to those of nonaffected people after appropriate treatment.

So far, however, only one type of psychotherapy has been found to be effective in the treatment of OCD. Treatment outcome research has shown that adults and children alike benefit from CBT, specifically a form of CBT that focuses on exposure and ritual prevention (E/RP). (E/RP will be discussed in depth later in the chapter.) Like medication, CBT has its own advantages and disadvantages.

The major advantages of CBT for OCD are as follows:

◊ CBT involves learning new behaviors. Patients develop skills that they can continue to use long after treatment ends, to keep their OCD weak and to prevent relapse.

◊ CBT is time-limited. The active phase of OCD treatment usually lasts for twelve to twenty sessions unless the child's condition is complicated by other disorders or a reluctance to participate.

◊ In the long run, CBT can end up being much less expensive than medication. Since the treatment takes place over the course of a few weeks or months rather than years, the cost is limited to that time period and does not go on and on.

◊ CBT can enhance self-esteem and confidence. Successful mastery of the skills taught in treatment and gaining control over symptoms can potentially boost a child's pride, self-esteem, and sense of competence, turning a difficult situation into a boon.

As promising as all this is, CBT treatment for OCD does not come without disadvantages:

◊ CBT requires committed and concentrated effort. This is not a therapy in which just talking to someone makes you feel better. It requires challenging oneself and one's fears, changing behaviors, and working hard.

◊ CBT requires time. Instead of taking a few seconds a day to swallow one's medication dose, CBT demands spending many hours every week during treatment on therapy sessions and daily homework between those sessions.

◊ Exposure and ritual prevention, the core techniques of CBT treatment for OCD, actually *cause* distress, albeit temporary. This is by far the most unpleasant aspect of CBT. E/RP therapy requires seeking out experiences that generate high levels of anxiety. You can think of it as investing anxiety and distress now to get peace and freedom in the future. Those who benefit from the therapy almost always feel that the investment has been worth it. Unfortunately, some feel unable to follow this difficult course and don't complete the treatment.

◊ Successful treatment often necessitates changes within the family. Sometimes the changes required are welcomed and sometimes they are not. More will be said on family-related issues in part 3 of this book.

◊ Finally, E/RP therapy is often not readily available. This is a specialized treatment, in which many mental health professionals (even many CBT practitioners) are not yet trained. Despite the yearly Behavior Therapy Institutes intensive workshops offered by the Obsessive-Compulsive Foundation to train mental health professionals, many areas of the country still have no local E/RP practitioners.

Option 3: Both Medication and Psychotherapy

Many lay people and professionals alike consider the benefits of both forms of treatment and think, "Well, if both work effectively on their own, then surely the best treatment plan would incorporate both." So, as you might expect, using both treatments together appears to be the most common approach in areas where both are available. However, clinical research has not yet consistently shown that combining treatments works better than using the individual treatments separately. So it remains an open question whether combining the treatments is truly advantageous. Many clinicians believe that combining the treatments can make CBT for OCD more doable, especially for patients with additional problems (see below). They argue that research so far has not captured the benefits to people with multiple problems (e.g., OCD with anxiety or depression) because these patients are often excluded from studies and clinical trials. Many patients report benefits from combining the treatments. Following are advantages of taking this approach:

◊ Since SRIs and SSRIs are also antidepressants, they can restore the energy and drive that many depressed OCD patients need in order to do E/RP. This is not an uncommon problem—having OCD is often depressing.

◊ Many people with OCD also experience a lot of general anxiety, and many are even afraid of their own anxiety. Since SRIs and SSRIs also reduce general anxiousness (and, in some cases, panic), they can make it easier for some OCD patients to tackle E/RP and engage in behaviors that are the equivalent of asking, "Could I please have some more anxiety?"

Disadvantages of combining the treatments include the following:

◊ For a minority of patients, the medication works just well enough to reduce their belief that they need E/RP but still leaves them significantly distressed or dysfunctional—better, but still badly affected by OCD.

◊ With both treatments in use, it can be difficult to determine what is and what is not working properly, particularly when the two treatments are started around the same time. If a patient improves, is it due to the medication or the CBT? If there's a setback, is it due to a medication problem or a difficulty with the CBT? Not knowing what is responsible for which results can complicate treatment. A patient who experiences a setback might decide to stop CBT until he finds the right medication or the right dose. Another patient who believes improvement is largely due to medication may be less likely to use her CBT tools later to fight a relapse.

Professional Guidelines

Because the decision is complex, a group of OCD experts came up with the Expert Consensus Treatment Guidelines for Obsessive-Compulsive Disorder to help professionals provide recommendations for effective treatment (March et al. 1997). Ultimately, parents are responsible for making the treatment choice, but you may find it useful to read these guidelines:

◊ Children who are not yet adolescents should be treated first with CBT alone. Medication should only be added if the CBT does not result in significant gains or if the child opposes engaging in CBT.

◊ For adolescents, CBT should still be the first line of treatment for those with milder OCD. For adolescents with more severe OCD, using the combined treatment from the start is recommended.

What to Expect from Your Chosen Treatment Strategy

Whichever treatment strategy you choose, it will be important for you as a parent to know what that strategy should look like. You will want to know that your child is receiving the right treatment, that it is being delivered correctly, and that it is working as intended. You don't want to put your child through any unnecessary distress nor do you want to waste valuable time or resources. What follows is a review of what to expect from the two individual treatment strategies, starting with medications.

Understanding the Medication

Many of the concerns that parents have about medications can be alleviated when they understand what to expect and when, what the risks are, and what to do about any problems that might develop. For this reason, discussing these issues with your psychiatrist and your pharmacist is very important. Make copies of the following Medication Profile and complete one each time your child is prescribed a new medication, to help you ask the relevant questions.

Arriving at the "Right" Medication

Finding the right medication and the right dose means keeping a delicate balance between achieving the desired therapeutic benefits and minimizing unwanted side effects. Prescribing medication is not an exact science. All the SRIs and SSRIs affect serotonin, but each does so a bit differently and comes with its own possible side effects. Additionally, every person is unique, so responses to medication can be unique as well.

Medication Profile

Medication: _____ Target therapeutic dose: _____

Date prescribed: _____ Dose and frequency: _____

Symptom(s) the medication will target: _____

How does this medication work? _____

_____

How long does it usually take for a patient to see positive effects? _____

What are the side effects of the medication? _____

_____

Are any side effects dangerous? Which ones should I report immediately? _____

_____

_____

What can I do to reduce the severity of side effects? _____

_____

My child is also taking (list other medications): _____

_____

Are there any potential drug interactions I should know about? _____

Are there any over-the-counter medications my child should avoid because of potential drug interactions? _____

My child has (list other medical conditions): _____

Is there any reason to think this medication will have an impact on these problems? _____

Are there any dietary restrictions for patients taking this medication? _____

_____

Do you have printed information about this medication? _____

(Ask your pharmacist, too. Many pharmacies give written information with every prescription. Take the time to read it, even if your doctor and pharmacist have explained the medication to you.)

Will my child need any tests before starting this medication or while taking it? If so, how often? _____

_____

_____

Chart 4a

Unfortunately, unwanted side effects also tend to be the first effects produced by these drugs. However, they usually lessen after a few weeks of taking the medication, it's important to try to help your child get through this stage. We will provide you with advice on managing some common side effects later in the chapter.

Your child may have to try more than one medication before arriving at the right one. In deciding which to try first, your child's psychiatrist will take into account potential side effects, your child's other medical needs, additional medications being taken, and previous responses of both your child and other family members to medications.

Antidepressants are generally started at a low dose and increased gradually to a targeted therapeutic dose, the dosage that is known to promote a favorable response in most people. It is always a good idea to ask what the target therapeutic dose is for your child. In most cases, it takes a full four to six weeks after reaching that therapeutic dose, which can itself take a considerable period of time, before deciding to try something else. Without an adequate trial, psychiatrists cannot conclude with certainty that the medication is a poor fit. In some circumstances, discontinuing a medication too soon could lead to having to try that same drug all over again at a later date.

Accurate Record Keeping

We believe it is important to keep accurate records of your child's medication history. The process of finding the right medication may be easy—the first medication you try may produce the desired response in your child. However, the situation could become complicated, with your child needing to try multiple medications before discovering one that works. Your child may only have a partial response to any of the medications, so the psychiatrist may suggest adding other medications to boost therapeutic effects. Side effects to one or more of the medications may emerge, which then require other medications to alleviate the negative effects. Still other problems may become evident, requiring additional medication strategies. When these complicated scenarios emerge, the situation can become confusing very quickly. If this happens, you will want an accurate record so that if you decide to change doctors you will not have to repeat costly trials of medications that you think did not work.

To help, we've developed a Medication Log for recording the relevant information. Make many copies of the blank form and complete a new log each week your child takes the medication. Write the number of weeks that each medication has been taken. Record each medication prescribed on a separate line, along with the present dose and the targeted therapeutic dose. In the column labeled "Target symptom," indicate the reason for the medication being prescribed (such as anxiety, depression, or obsessions). Use the five-point rating scale to indicate any changes to that symptom you have noticed. Then rate the overall effect of your child's combination of medications on anxiety, depression, anger, and ability to engage in therapy. A note of caution: When the medication scenario is not routine (your child has not experienced the desired response with the first or second medication tried), we strongly recommend that you work with a psychiatrist (preferably an

OCD expert) rather than a general practitioner. The needs of children with OCD can be complex, and so you will need a doctor who is very familiar with psychiatric drugs.

Managing Unwanted Side Effects

Keep your child's prescribing doctor aware of side effects that develop. If you have doubts about a symptom, don't hesitate to ask the doctor if it could be related to the medication. Doctors can usually adjust dosages or have your child take the medication at a different time to minimize side effects. Do not halt the medication or make any changes without consulting the doctor. If it should be stopped, it will probably need to be discontinued gradually. Abrupt withdrawal from some medications, such as clomipramine (Anafranil), can cause severe reactions.

It is quite common for children to experience some mild side effects at first. Be ready for them. Below, we've provided you with some recommendations for managing some of the most commonly seen side effects so that you can help your child hang in there while his or her body adjusts to the new medication.

- ◊ Bedtime struggles: OCD medications can make children sleepy or make them feel so restless that they can't sleep. If you notice either of these side effects, ask the doctor if the dosage times can be adjusted. Taking activating medications earlier can make it easier to fall asleep at bedtime, and taking sedating ones before bed can help prevent sleepiness during the day. Developing a soothing bedtime routine, such as turning off the TV and reading stories, can also help your child relax and get to sleep.

- ◊ Weight fluctuations: Some people lose weight on SRIs (at least initially), but many more gain weight. If weight fluctuations are severe, medication can be changed. The best approach is to expect weight changes and take precautions by being especially vigilant about maintaining a healthy diet and exercise program. However, don't single out your child with OCD; make health and fitness a family project.

- ◊ Dry mouth: Medication can reduce saliva, causing the mouth to become dry. Sipping fluids frequently, chewing gum, and sucking on hard candies can help. Saliva helps fight plaque, so pay special attention to dental care. Consult with your child's dentist regarding this issue.

- ◊ Nausea or heartburn: Taking medication with meals or with a small amount of food can prevent nausea. If heartburn is a problem, it's best not to lie down for a couple hours after eating or taking the medicine. Placing an extra pillow under your child's head can relieve nighttime heartburn.

- ◊ Constipation or diarrhea: Exercising, drinking plenty of fluids, and eating high-fiber foods (such as raw vegetables, fruits, and whole grains) can help relieve constipation. Drinking plenty of fluids (to avoid dehydration), avoiding high-fiber foods, and eating low-fiber foods can help relieve diarrhea. Notify the doctor if

Medication Log

Date: _____

Rating Scale

1	2	3	4	5
much improved	improved	no change	worse	much worse

Number of weeks taken	Medication	Current dose	Therapeutic dose	Target symptom	Target symptom effect (rate 1 to 5)

Weekly Ratings

Anxiety	Depression	Anger	Ability to engage in therapy	Unwanted side effects:
				Other observations:

Chart 4b

diarrhea is persistent or severe or if you notice signs of dehydration, such as dizziness, weakness, fever, or decreased urine output.

◊ Behavioral side effects: Some children will experience hyperactivity, restlessness, drowsiness, anxiety, or even aggressive behavior while taking medications for OCD. These side effects often subside after taking the medication for a while. However, the presence of other disorders and the addition of new medications sometimes make it difficult to tell what is causing behavioral changes. Your medication log will help the prescribing doctor decide whether symptoms are the result of medication and if dosage changes are in order. Always notify your child's doctor of extreme mood or behavioral changes, especially if there appears to be a threat of danger to self or others.

Understanding CBT Treatment for OCD

CBT is a broad field that encompasses many therapeutic techniques, not all of which are useful in the treatment of OCD. This section will explain what your child will need from therapy, how the appropriate therapy works for adults, and how this therapy is adapted for use with children.

The term *cognitive behavioral therapy* refers to therapy that merges and utilizes the theories and techniques of two separate traditions: cognitive therapy and behavior therapy. Cognitive therapy grew out of research into thinking and it proposes that by changing the way you think you can change how you feel and behave. Behavior therapy grew out of research into learning and proposes that by changing how you behave you can change the way you feel and think. Since the underlying assumptions of these two therapeutic approaches are so similar (both proposing that thinking, actions, and behavior are inter-related), their techniques are generally complementary and compatible.

However, therapists who identify themselves as cognitive behavioral therapists can use vastly different techniques and approaches. You could say that CBT forms a contin-uum with pure cognitive therapy at one end and pure behavior therapy at the other. Some cognitive behavioral therapists are primarily cognitive in their approach and others primar-ily behavioral, with the majority of CBT therapists falling somewhere in between. What they emphasize, how they approach problems, and what techniques they rely on can vary greatly, often depending on their approach and the techniques they have mastered.

What this means for you is that simply hiring a therapist who identifies him- or her-self as cognitive behavioral does not necessarily mean that your child will receive the appropriate treatment for OCD. Receiving inappropriate treatment can occur because some CBT techniques are contraindicated for OCD and can even make the OCD worse. One example is thought suppression. In chapter 1, we discussed thought suppression, a method of mental avoidance commonly used by people with OCD to block intrusive thoughts. But thought suppression or *thought stopping,* is also a CBT technique, one that is used effectively to treat certain other disorders, including depression and anger problems.

In fact, it used to be used for OCD before it became clear that it did not work. Some cognitive behavioral therapists still attempt to treat OCD with this strategy—to their clients' detriment.

Only one CBT approach, with two specific behavioral techniques at its core, has been proven to reduce the symptoms of OCD. These two essential techniques together are called *exposure and ritual prevention* (also known as *response prevention*) or E/RP. Other CBT techniques may be used in the treatment, but they should not be the heart of the therapy. The purpose of using other CBT techniques should be to support the E/RP exercises or to address coexisting problems (such as depression or anger). More will be said about the proper and improper use of other CBT techniques later.

The Big Guns of Treatment: Exposure and Ritual Prevention

Alleviating the discomfort of a person with OCD requires increasing that person's tolerance for uncertainty or risk and reducing sensitivity to his or her "triggers" (cues of danger or discomfort). This is accomplished by using exposure and ritual prevention, the big guns for OCD. Exposure involves intentionally confronting situations that cause anxiety, fear, or distress. Ritual prevention involves voluntarily abstaining from the rituals that provide relief. Doing these two new behaviors together is equivalent to practicing acceptance and tolerance of uncertainty. Basically the term "exposure and ritual prevention" is a fancy way of saying, "Practice doing what you are afraid of, and practice not doing what makes you feel better." The eventual result is that the person with OCD ends up feeling less threatened by the obsessive concerns that were previously so disturbing.

Why Does E/RP Work?

Before one can understand how or why E/RP works, one must first understand that the thoughts, feelings, and behaviors of OCD are overlearned responses. Consider the following scenario: A boy with OCD who is afraid of contamination enters a doctor's office and sees a "trigger," a used and crumpled tissue on the coffee table. He carefully sits down, folds his arms across his chest with his hands under his arms, and moves his knees carefully so he will not touch the table, much less the tissue.

What overlearned responses have occurred? The first response is to have the obsessive thought at the sight of the trigger: crumpled tissue—*germs!* The second response is to feel distressed by the thought: germs—*anxiety!* The third response is to avoid the tissue to minimize further distress: anxiety—avoidance—*relief!* If the boy had not been able to practice avoidance because the doctor shook his hand while holding the tissue, then he would probably have had a fourth response, to perform a ritual to get relief: wash—*relief!* Note that some of these overlearned responses are involuntary and automatic (having the obsessive thought and feeling distressed), while others (avoiding and rituals) are volitional and intentional.

E/RP works because repeatedly practicing new volitional behaviors gradually replaces the old volitional, overlearned responses, establishing new behavioral response patterns. This process is like building a new railroad junction so a train can follow a new track. Using E/RP creates a junction. The more E/RP is practiced, the stronger the junction becomes because practice can make almost anything easier to do. Thus, voluntarily rehearsing confronting scary situations and resisting rituals helps to make these choices easier as well.

However, it's not just repeated practice that makes the new behaviors easier to do. The new junction created by E/RP opens the person up to new experiences, allowing him or her to build a new track for healthy automatic responses (feeling okay in the presence of obsessions and having them infrequently) to replace the old OCD track (feeling distressed by obsessions and having them frequently). In building this new track, the first ties to be laid are changes to the distress response: the person becomes able to have the intrusive thought without feeling so upset. As distress in response to the thought diminishes, resisting the rituals becomes easier to do. More ties are added, carrying the track farther away from the old way of responding. When distress is lowered substantially, and rituals are easily resisted, the intrusive thoughts then begin to occur less frequently. Eventually, as the distress becomes minimal or even nonexistent, the track branches far off from the original, and the obsessive response when confronting a trigger may disappear entirely.

Helping to build this new track are the new experiences of feeling anxiety diminish in the presence of a trigger and discovering that predicted catastrophes rarely occur. When a person with OCD confronts a fearful trigger without ritualizing, he or she usually sits and waits for something terrible to happen—for the anxiety to spin out of control and for some disaster to occur. The new experience that occurs instead is . . . nothing. The anxiety dissipates and life continues without the predicted disaster. The person has the novel experience of feeling in control despite the presence of the feared trigger and the intrusive obsessions.

These new experiences occur for two reasons. First, catastrophes rarely occur because the obsessions are truly "false alarms" that warn of high risk when risk is actually low. Therefore, risk taking under these circumstances is not very risky. Second, alarms eventually shut off when proven false. It turns out that the human nervous system is hardwired both to create a fight or flight alarm when threat is perceived and to restore a calm state when there's no imminent danger. The calming process is called habituation. Habituation opposes the body's alarm and works in concert with it. When a threat is perceived, the alarm rings. When the danger is dealt with or if no danger materializes, then habituation occurs. Both processes are automatic and largely involuntary; you don't need to do anything to make them happen.

Habituation affords the experience of feeling calm in a situation that previously was falsely considered threatening. It is a psychologically powerful process because it can change a person's involuntary fearful response. When habituation occurs because no danger has materialized and the body has calmed down, being calm and safe is associated with the fearful trigger, weakening its previous association with fear. These are the ties of the new track. Habituation is the swinging sledgehammer that anchors the ties in place. Each time safety is experienced in the presence of the fearful trigger, each time an E/RP exercise is practiced, a new railroad tie is laid. The next time that fearful trigger is encountered, the involuntary response is less fearful. This reduced distress makes the person's next choice to confront a fear and resist a ritual easier to accomplish.

The power of E/RP does not stop there. E/RP also promotes an understanding of anxiety and of one's own coping abilities. Individuals discover that they, in fact, are strong enough to confront uncertainty and outlast their own anxious responding. They additionally learn that they do not need to do anything but persevere, because anxiety goes down on its own as long as they are willing to sit it out. Finally, they can feel and believe what their intellect has known all along, that avoiding and ritualizing do not really provide safety after all. This understanding helps courage and confidence grow, making it progressively easier to accept and tolerate uncertainty.

What Does E/RP Look Like?

So how does E/RP work in practice? In the example of the boy in the doctor's office, two separate E/RP exercises might be designed to have the boy (1) deliberately touch and contaminate his hands and body with the used tissue (confronting or exposing himself to the fearful situation), and (2) actively imagine and elaborate on the idea of becoming contaminated and then becoming very sick (confronting or exposing himself to the fearful idea). These exposure exercises would be practiced while actively choosing not to perform any ritual or safety behavior.

What would happen? The boy would feel anxious for a while, but after some time had elapsed, the anxiety would drop because his nervous system would register safety. Used tissues and thoughts of becoming sick would then feel somewhat less scary. Additionally, he would come to appreciate that he could confront the fearful situation and resist engaging in the safety behavior and still survive, and that would make it easier for him to confront and resist at a later time. Would the problem be cured? No. The distressing feeling, desire to avoid, and urge to wash would be weakened but not removed. Unfortunately, there can be no cure, because learning can never be erased, only weakened and overshadowed by something more strongly learned.

The process described above does not happen quickly. It has taken a lot of practice to establish the responses of OCD, and it requires just as much practice to make them weak and establish new responses. However, with each repetition of the new responses, the peak distress becomes a little less intense and diminishes a little faster. As anxiety drops, the choices to confront and resist become progressively easier to make. Eventually, little to no distress is evoked by the intrusive thought. Sometimes the obsessive thoughts even become less frequent or disappear; the person no longer cares whether he or she has the intrusive thought because it now seems so unimportant.

The Process of Therapy

In preparing to do E/RP, one first creates a list of triggers for obsessive thoughts. The most comprehensive way to build such a list is to include everything that the person avoids because it might prompt an obsession and everything that person does that leads to a ritual. The patient then works with the therapist to rate each trigger on the list using a personal subjective units of distress scale (SUDS). This scale ranges from 0 (no distress) to 100 (panic/terror). Then the rated items are ordered according to rank from least distressing to most distressing.

This list (called an exposure hierarchy) then becomes the blueprint for treatment. With the therapist's support and modeling, the patient will confront each fear trigger on the list while abstaining from rituals. The patient and therapist start with in-session exposures, working on the easier, less anxiety-provoking items in early sessions, and gradually working up to the most difficult items in later sessions. Between sessions, the person practices these and related exercises at home.

To increase the likelihood that an exercise will be beneficial, the therapist should *not* assure the patient of safety. Remember that the person is trying to establish a new practice of accepting uncertainty and risk. Receiving guarantees of safety would work against these efforts. Additionally, to be successful, the exercise must continue until the distress has dropped significantly. Exercises that are stopped prematurely, before habituation occurs, are similar to avoidance and do not promote the necessary new associations of safety with the triggers. Finally, the exercises must be repeated many times.

To achieve success, the individual must practice both exposure *and* response prevention. Often individuals will want to do one or the other but not both, but research has shown that this doesn't work. Exposure without ritual prevention may initially strengthen the ability to accept uncertainty, but the fearful response to the intrusive thought and the urge to ritualize remain just as strong because the person at some point performs the ritual. If ritual prevention occurs without exposure, the absence of confronting fears allows avoidance behaviors to continue. In both cases, safety is wrongly attributed to safety behaviors and the desired new association between the fearful trigger and safety is not strengthened.

Some people will draw a line in the sand, saying they will work on some areas of their OCD, but that other areas of obsessive concern are off-limits. Leaving areas of OCD unaddressed is usually a kiss of death for the outcome. Very simply, what is not worked on does not improve. What does not improve usually grows and spreads like cancer. Before too long, the person is back to his or her old ways.

Similarly, people often do not want to tackle extreme exposures. A patient might say, "Okay, I'll touch a dirty tissue, but don't ask me to touch old, dirty chewing gum stuck to the bottom of a table and then eat a cookie." These folks want their exposure exercises to approximate normal life and hope that this will bring their behavior into the normal range. Unfortunately, this strategy doesn't work.

One problem with this strategy is that if someone only works with ordinary triggers, he or she may get some temporary relief but will generally be comfortable only in the particular situations that were practiced. Progress in this approach to therapy comes very slowly because the person must practice every possible problem situation. The main advantage of working with extreme exposures is that it makes most ordinary everyday situations seem easy in comparison. Progress comes quickly because the feeling of being safe generalizes to many situations instead of just to the situation that was practiced. The other problem with working only with ordinary triggers is that one could never come up with every possibility that the world might offer. So, the person is set up to relapse. Encountering new situations in the course of everyday life is inevitable. These unpracticed normal situations will then trigger the old uncertainty and distress. The person will again want to avoid and ritualize. Thus, in order to reduce anxiety sufficiently to feel comfortable in most ordinary situations and to guard against relapse, the patient must become comfortable in situations that go beyond normal. When patients practice inviting uncertainty by confronting extreme situations, then most normal situations seem relatively safe and doable in comparison.

Proper and Improper Use of Other CBT Techniques for OCD

In certain cases, other CBT techniques are sometimes used in the treatment of OCD. Depending on the patient's needs and type of OCD, these treatment strategies may or may not be effective. For some people with OCD, the techniques may actually hinder the treatment process. Below is a discussion of these alternative techniques.

Cognitive Restructuring

Cognitive restructuring (CR) techniques are CBT strategies that were developed from cognitive therapy. These techniques teach the patient to identify problematic thoughts or beliefs and then to objectively evaluate and challenge those thoughts. This process generally results in the patient adopting less extreme thoughts or less problematic beliefs.

Proper use of CR in the treatment of OCD should be limited to supporting E/RP strategies (Grayson 2003). Using CR to lower anxiety is not productive for most OCD patients because they already recognize that their thoughts are unrealistic and that the situation is probably safe. Their problem is not that they do not know a situation is probably safe, it's that it doesn't *feel* safe. Because they overvalue the feeling of alarm, they choose to disregard their rational evaluation. Often CR works for a little while because it strengthens what they already know, but because the technique does not bridge the gap between rational understanding and felt experience, the doubt resurfaces. Many times, the result is that the cognitive restructuring activity itself becomes a ritual.

Think of it in the following way. If someone were to attach electrodes to you, plug them in, ring a buzzer and flash lights, and then shock you badly, you would experience pain. If this was repeated multiple times, you would learn to be afraid of the buzzer and the flashing lights because your body would have learned that lights and noise signify imminent pain. If the electrodes were unpluged in front of you, you would then know intellectually that you were safe because the electrodes were unplugged. However, if the buzzer was again rung and the lights flashed, you would still startle and feel afraid. Of course, this fear reaction is not rational. But you are predisposed to form associations between stimuli, and you have learned that the light and buzzer are dangerous, and so your body reacts with fear. No amount of cognitive restructuring will change this reaction, because it's not a thinking problem. It's a problem of learned fear. To weaken this learning, one would need to hear the buzzer and see the lights many times without being shocked. This would reestablish a calm response or "safety" association to the buzzer and lights—in other words, exposure (Grayson 2003).

However, CR can be useful, or even necessary, for those OCD patients who actually believe that their behaviors are necessary. These people believe that their "false alarms" are real. In these situations, the goal of CR is to help them rationally evaluate a situation so that they can know it's safe even though it feels like it's not. These folks are then well situated to begin E/RP.

OCD patients can also use CR to help them challenge the common OCD beliefs that anxiety is dangerous and too painful to experience. These beliefs can interfere with an individual's willingness to undertake E/RP therapy. CR can help people appreciate that they have strength enough to withstand E/RP.

CR is also useful to promote a feeling of helplessness with regard to fearful situations. This may sound like a strange goal, but Dr. Jon Grayson and Dr. Fitzgibbons think that the mistaken belief that supports OCD in almost every affected person is that unacceptable outcomes are or should be avoidable and controllable. As long as individuals believe that somehow, if they just do it right, they can control an unwanted experience, they will remain invested in their avoidance and compulsions. Using CR to challenge this belief promotes the recognition that efforts at attaining certainty (such as ritualizing) are futile because certainty does not exist. We are all, to some extent, helpless. When people realize this, and allow themselves to feel helpless, then they are better situated to abandon their rituals.

Externalizing OCD (It's Not Me; It's the OCD!)

This cognitive technique was popularized primarily by the book *Brain Lock* by Jeffrey Schwartz and Beverly Beyette (1996). The idea is to teach people to distance themselves from anxious thoughts, recognize that obsessions differ from personal beliefs, and dismiss the concerns as "just OCD thoughts." This strategy sometimes helps people to disbelieve the false alarms so that they can resist performing rituals and continue with normal activity. Additionally, for many people this strategy reduces shame about the obsessions.

A possible cost to this strategy is that the technique can backfire because it does not promote the acceptance of uncertainty. Some people with OCD use the "that's just OCD" line to convince themselves that there is no risk. They feel somewhat better after convincing themselves, but not so much so that they confront the risk. For example, a teenager might actively dismiss violent obsessions as "just OCD" when eating dinner with his or her family but continue to use a butter knife to cut steak. Risk avoidance remains intact, and the obsessive fear is not weakened.

Anxiety-Management Techniques (AMT)

Progressive muscle relaxation and breathing retraining are rarely used in the treatment of OCD. These techniques are generally counterproductive because their implicit message is contrary to the lessons of E/RP. A major take-home message of E/RP is that anxiety is not dangerous and does not need to be controlled because it passes on its own. The take-home message of AMT is that anxiety should be controlled and this is how to do it. In addition, for some people, AMT techniques can become new rituals.

Situations where clinicians *sometimes* believe this risk is worth taking include the following: when panic attacks occur during exposure work; when high anxiety prevents a patient from attempting E/RP exercises; and when anger flares during E/RP. Even in these situations, using AMT may be problematic and should be phased out as soon as possible.

Adapting E/RP for Children

So how does E/RP work with children? Basically, the same way it works with adults. Although E/RP was originally developed for adults, it is also the key to successful outcomes for children. However, adaptations are made to render the treatment more child-friendly.

Externalizing the OCD (Naming the Bully)

The "It's the OCD, not me!" technique discussed earlier is emphasized more with children because of its advantages in the treatment of children. As with adults, it can lessen the shame and encourage resisting rituals during an OC moment. More important, this strategy changes the dynamics of the problem within the family.

When children have OCD, children and parents frequently struggle against each other. To protect him- or herself and hide the OCD, the child fights with the parent. To force normal functioning, the parents fight the child. Externalizing the OCD can lessen this struggle. The child and parents can work together to fight a common enemy, the OCD.

For children, externalizing OCD often means dubbing it a "bully" and actually naming it (March and Mulle 1998). Naming the bully accomplishes many things: it invites added distance; it affords an opportunity to give silly (or insulting) names to the bully, which serve to put the child in the position of superiority over the OCD; and it sets up the idea that if you stand up to it the bully will back down. The metaphor of the bully also makes the disorder more understandable to a child because OCD really does act like a bully: it lies; it tries to make kids do things they don't want to do; if the kids do these things, it wants more; and it pretends to be a friend when it really isn't.

The Game Metaphor

Treatment for children is often couched as a game where the opponent being played is OCD. This metaphor also helps children and their families to externalize the OCD and strengthens the idea that people need to work together to help the child recover. It also provides a vocabulary for treatment that is readily understandable to parents and children alike and clarifies roles and expectations for the therapy process. Finally, the metaphor affords opportunities to make some of the more tedious aspects of E/RP appealing to children. Rather than monitor rituals and avoidance, children "spy on the OCD." Rather than create a hierarchy, children create maps to show what territory the OCD controls, what the child controls, and what is still up for grabs.

The Wish List

Most therapists who work with children with OCD use some sort of wish list. That is, they urge and sometimes help parents to develop a reinforcement strategy with their child that will encourage the child to stay involved in the therapeutic process. This strategy usually incorporates receiving "stuff" of one kind or another. We'll discuss this more in part 3.

The Fear Thermometer

Having a means of communicating levels of distress is necessary for treatment. The SUDS scale used with adults is made child-friendly by transforming it into a "fear thermometer." This metaphor helps children understand the concept that distress is continuous rather than an all-or-nothing experience. The tool is useful in treatment planning, doing exercises in therapy sessions, and helping family members communicate and make decisions during OC moments at home. Parents can ask, "What's your temperature?" to get a sense of their child's distress. Children can answer and have some confidence that they will be understood.

Exposure Exercises

Exposure has the same goals, works the same way, and needs to be implemented following the same principles with children as with adults. The difference is that when treating children the therapist needs to make it fun, possibly in the form of games or creative art projects. For children thirteen or under, if the task is not somehow engaging they won't want to continue coming to therapy. The need to make the exercises fun becomes less important as the child matures. Exposure exercises for most teenagers look pretty much like what an adult would be asked to do.

Ritual Prevention

With kids, ritual prevention is more gradual than it is with adults. Therapists generally focus on one ritual at a time, and children are frequently eased into stopping by being encouraged to delay a ritual or change a ritual, helping them to notice that they do have some control while they warm to the idea of stopping. However, stopping all rituals completely remains the goal. It's important that the delays and changes represent steps, not plateaus. When these tactics are used for too long, delay can train the child to stay anxious, and changed rituals can wind up being substituted for old rituals.

Cultivating detachment is a ritual-prevention tactic often used with children. It consists of training the child to passively ignore the obsession without doing anything about it. Think of it as learning to tolerate having the radio on a station you don't like without trying to change it. The child learns to not interact with the obsession at all. The goal isn't to turn the thought off, suppress it, or argue with it, but to let it drone on as though it doesn't matter. When Dr. Fitzgibbons teaches this to children, she has a puppet intermittently say random terrible things during the session. Eventually, she and the child both stop paying attention to the puppet's comments.

Another form of ritual prevention used with children is called "bossing it back." Actually, this term refers to a few tactics used with children, but basically the response-prevention part of "bossing OCD back" is to respond to an OC obsession and urge to ritualize by saying something like "I'll show you I'm boss! I won't do what you want!" When a child is really progressing well, ritual prevention can take the form of an exposure instead of the ritual, just to show the fear who is truly boss: "You say I'll fail if I don't study more. I'll take that risk! I'm going out with my friends!"

Other Forms of Bossing Back OCD (Cognitive Techniques)

Cognitive restructuring aimed at risk assessment is done more frequently with children because they are less likely than adults to realize that their behaviors are irrational or unnecessary. The goal, as with adults with poor insight, is to foster a rational understanding that contradicts the fear, not to alleviate anxiety by persuading the child that the situation is safe. In Dr. Fitzgibbons's work with children, she calls this risk assessment "building two voices," referring to building up the child's own voice to disagree with the OCD.

Another useful cognitive exercise for children is learning positive coping talk. Children with OCD often hesitate to do E/RP or to undertake other challenges because they feel bad about themselves. They're thinking a lot of negative things about themselves and their abilities. Dr. Fitzgibbons tries to catch negative self-talk and refers to it as the bully's efforts to "psych them out" so they won't play as well. Children practice talking back to the OCD, incorporating positive statements and countering the OCD's putdowns.

The final bossing-back technique is to deliberately make fun of the bully. Laughing at the OCD helps children feel in charge. Generally, the more humor the better. However, this strategy can backfire with children who believe that people are laughing at them. The solution is to always follow the child's lead.

Anxiety-Management Techniques

Relaxation techniques are used more frequently with children than they are with adults. Their emotional immaturity leaves them needing more help learning how to deal with strong emotions. Panic, anger, and aggressive behavior are much more likely to occur in high-distress moments, so children need to learn ways to moderate their negative emotions. However, clinicians still need to be careful when they use these techniques, because overuse with children carries the same risks as it does with adults.

In this chapter we have discussed treatment options and how to choose the right treatment. We have discussed medication therapy and cognitive behavioral therapy for OCD. Hopefully, you now have a much better understanding of the terms and concepts involved and what your child needs. Now that you are equipped with information and may even know what you are looking for, we will discuss how to find the help you need.

Chapter 5

Getting Started

Now that you know something about treatment, it is time to find someone to help your child. But first you'll want to get your child involved. If your child has come to you and asked for help, then your only problem is finding the right experts. Getting children to seek help when they have not admitted a problem can be difficult. Before making an appointment, discuss your concerns with your child. Broach the subject gently without diagnosing the problem yourself. Explain that you think it might be helpful for your child to talk to someone who might know of some things he or she can do to help. What you are trying to do is to create a safe space for your child to talk more about their difficulties. If you minimize the problem and the importance of the appointment, it will make the whole process less threatening to your child, who may still be invested in completely hiding the OCD.

With children who have asked for help already or who respond to the idea of getting help by opening up and talking freely about their difficulties, the parent's task is easier. Explain what you have learned about OCD in a nonjudgmental and accepting way. Many children are often extremely relieved to hear that there is a name for this problem. You might compare OCD to diabetes or poor vision, and getting help for OCD to taking insulin or getting eyeglasses. If your child reveals feeling ashamed about having this problem, point out that nearly everybody has some problem to deal with. Provide examples of difficulties that your extended family and friends have. Finally, remind your child that, whatever the assessment and treatment plan, you view getting help as a family endeavor, which you will be working on together. Emphasize acceptance of his or her difficulties, interest in his or her experiences, and hopefulness about the treatment options available.

Sometimes parents attempt to avoid conflict by bringing a child for an assessment interview without explaining where they are going or why. Such a strategy usually leaves a child confused and angry and can cause the child to deny his or her problems. Furthermore, since cooperation is essential to treatment, such a tactic starts the entire process off on the wrong foot. It's best to let your child know that you are making an appointment to see someone, and inform him or her of the reason for the appointment.

How to Find an Expert

Your first stop should be your child's pediatrician. If your child is not severely distressed or impaired, you prefer that your child receives medication treatment, and your pediatrician is willing to prescribe an appropriate medication, you may be able to stop there. Some pediatricians are knowledgeable about OCD and are comfortable treating OCD patients medically. In mild or uncomplicated cases, this practice can work out well because the parent and child probably already have a trusting relationship with the doctor.

If your child is quite distressed or the problem appears more severe, you may need someone with more OCD expertise. Start with the pediatrician's recommendations of mental health professionals who specialize in treating OCD. Pediatricians regularly refer patients to child psychiatrists and psychologists and often hear back from their patients and parents about their experiences with these professionals—whether the treatment helped, whether the clinician had a child-friendly manner, whether the clinician worked well with the parents, and so on. Hearing these reports from patients puts pediatricians in a position to provide excellent recommendations.

Another way to find names of local OCD specialists is to contact professional organizations. The Obsessive-Compulsive Foundation (OCF), the Obsessive Compulsive Information Center (Dean Foundation), the Anxiety Disorders Association of America (ADAA), and the Association for Advancement of Behavior Therapy (AABT) all maintain listings of mental health professionals who treat OCD. (Addresses for these groups are listed in Resources at the end of this book.) Keep in mind, however, that these professionals have identified *themselves* as experts. The organizations do not track what these professionals actually know or do. Being on a list does not necessarily mean that a clinician is right for your child, but it increases the odds.

Decide What Kind of Provider to Look For

If you are seeking medication treatment for your child, you will want to find a child psychiatrist. Psychiatrists are medical doctors who are trained to diagnose and treat disorders of the brain. Most of these folks do not know how to conduct cognitive behavioral therapy (CBT) because it's not part of their training. However, some have sought out additional training in CBT on their own. More important than whether a psychiatrist knows how to do CBT, however, is whether he or she is willing to support and work with a CBT therapist in case you decide later to add or switch to CBT.

If you are seeking psychotherapy, then you will want to look for a child psychologist, specifically one who knows how to treat OCD using exposure and ritual prevention (E/RP). A psychologist is your best bet because psychologists are more often trained in CBT and E/RP than other kinds of mental health therapists (e.g., social workers, psychiatric nurses, family therapists, or educational counselors). However, the key qualification is training in E/RP, and some people from other disciplines may have sought out additional training, making them experienced and qualified to provide E/RP. The real issue is not the therapist's degree but whether he or she has sufficient experience with E/RP and can form a strong alliance with your child.

Investigate Your Insurance Benefits

OCD treatment can get costly. You will probably want to take advantage of your insurance benefits, if you can. To identify a provider the company will pay for, compare your list of potential experts with your insurance company's list of authorized providers. You may find that the insurance company's list contains no experts, leaving you to choose between going "out of network" and footing the bill yourself or battling with your insurance company to get them to pay for an out-of-network provider. Sometimes, squeaky wheels do get the grease, and many individuals who duke it out with their insurance companies prevail. This choice takes great stamina and perseverance, and the cost in stress may not be worth it to you. The important thing is to keep your eye on your goal: getting the right treatment for your child. Not getting appropriate treatment can both prolong your child's problem and end up costing more money in the long run.

Avoid Unethical Providers

An unfortunate reality is that some providers engage in unethical practices. State licensing boards, which exist to protect the consumer, can usually provide information about disciplinary action taken against licensees. If you want to check on a clinician's license status, a good starting point would be to call your state government's general information number and ask for the licensing board for that clinician's profession (e.g., medicine, psychology, or social work). We have provided a line on the Psychiatrist and Therapist Interview forms at the end of this chapter for you to record information about the clinician's license, so that you can consider these issues when making your decision.

Interview Potential Providers

Once you have identified a few potential providers, start with a phone call to each provider. We have prepared forms to guide you in your interviews (these forms can be found at the end of this chapter. Make copies of the relevant form (either psychiatrist or therapist) and fill them out during your calls.

You will be looking for three kinds of information in each interview: business-related details, expertise, and personal style. For the business-related information, find out whether the person's costs and location match your needs. For expertise information, ask the questions as written and listen to hear whether the answers match the information we have provided about the types of effective treatments. Be careful not to feed the professional the correct response, asking questions such as "Do you use SSRIs?" or "Do you use E/RP?" Let the provider reveal his or her expertise to you. For personal information, listen for whether the person sounds like someone you might want to work with and your child might feel comfortable with. When you have completed your interviews, you will be prepared to decide who is likely to be a good match.

What to Expect in the First Few Sessions

It might be several weeks between your interview calls and your child's first appointment. You can use this time to observe and record your child's symptoms. Your child's clinician should welcome this information since assessment and diagnosis will be the main focus of these first sessions. Chapter 8 will help you compile records that will provide your child's therapist with valuable information and paint a more accurate picture of the symptoms.

Generally, the first session will involve not only questions about your child's problem but also background questions about your child's developmental history, educational functioning, social-emotional development, peer relationships, interests, medical issues, and family history. Often the provider will spend part of this session educating you about OCD and its treatment.

The second session will typically be devoted to a more detailed assessment of your child's OCD. Often, a standardized diagnostic interview, such as the Yale-Brown obsessive compulsive scale (Y-BOCS) for adults and teenagers or the child's version (CY-BOCS), will be used to identify specific symptoms and assess severity. These are also used to track and measure improvement of symptoms during treatment.

Don't be in too much of a hurry to get medication started. When taking their child to see a psychiatrist, some parents want to leave the initial visit with a prescription in hand, but that is not necessarily a good thing. A more thorough evaluation can prevent false starts on a wrong medication. So, attending a couple of sessions before a prescription is written can save time, money, and frustration in the long run.

The first couple of sessions will also be important because you may discover that you and your child are not satisfied after meeting the provider. The success of treatment (especially CBT) often hinges on an elusive thing called "chemistry" and the collaborative relationship that your child and the provider are able to forge. If your child dislikes the clinician, it is unlikely that the treatment will be a success. Be willing to keep looking until you find a qualified psychiatrist or therapist that your child can work with.

What to Do If You Cannot Find an Expert OCD Therapist

As we pointed out in chapter 4, one disadvantage of using psychotherapy is that you may have trouble finding mental health professionals in your area who are qualified to provide E/RP treatment. There are no great solutions to this problem, but here are some ideas.

First of all, you can adjust your definition of the word "local." Perhaps a competent therapist is available an hour (or two or three) from your home. This may seem like a waste of time spent driving, but compare it to the cost in time and money spent on therapy that does not work. You could also use vacation time and travel with your child to see an expert in another city who provides a three-week intensive outpatient program. Many experienced therapists who conduct these programs will find time in their schedule to accommodate such patients. These kinds of intensive programs generally consist of daily two-hour therapy sessions, with an average of three to four hours of therapy home-work each day. Some places (such as the Center for the Treatment and Study of Anxiety at the University of Pennsylvania in Philadelphia) routinely provide a three-week course of therapy because many of their clientele travel long distances to get there. However, you are probably not limited to such programs.

Another solution is to find a therapist who wants to learn E/RP treatment and is willing to work with you. This option does come with a big obstacle: any therapist who is beginning work with a new client population is obligated to find (and pay) a competent supervisor to guide him or her. Generally, the costs of supervision are equal to the costs for therapy itself. Therapists may not want to invest in such training. So, you may wonder, could you pay for that supervision (on top of session fees)? Probably not. Such an arrangement would place you in a dual role (patient and sponsor) that could violate the therapist's professional ethics by being potentially exploitative. So, although the therapist may need to get supervision in order to treat your child, he or she cannot expect you to pay for it. We suggest persuading the clinician that training would be worth the investment because it could create a lucrative new area of his or her practice.

If you find such a therapist, you can suggest that he or she contact the Obsessive-Compulsive Foundation to inquire about their next Behavior Therapy Institute. For more immediate assistance, you can recommend books that the therapist can consult to learn more about this therapy. We recommend the following:

- ◊ *OCD in Children and Adolescents: A Cognitive-Behavioral Treatment Manual* by John March and Karen Mulle. This is a treatment manual that instructs therapists in both the rationale of treatment and what to do for children on a session-by-session basis.

◊   *Mastery of Obsessive-Compulsive Disorder Therapist Guide* (Therapyworks Series) by Michael Kozak and Edna Foa, and *Overcoming Obsessive-Compulsive Disorder: A Behavioral and Cognitive Protocol for the Treatment of OCD (Therapist Protocol)* (Best Practices Series) by Gail S. Steketee. These books are intended to educate therapists in the treatment of OCD. Although they focus on the treatment of adults, the essential concepts of treatment that are necessary for successful treatment of OCD are covered very clearly. Thus, they provide excellent resources, even for therapists wanting to treat children with OCD.

◊   *The OCD Workbook: Your Guide to Breaking Free from Obsessive-Compulsive Disorder* by Bruce Hyman and Cherry Pedrick. This self-help book is written so that readers can use it alone or with the assistance of a therapist. It can be adapted for use with children.

If you cannot find either a seasoned E/RP therapist or an inexperienced therapist who is smart and eager to learn, you may feel tempted to learn and provide the therapy yourself. Let us be clear: We do not recommend this solution under any circumstances. However, we also recognize that this is an imperfect world, and some parents will believe they have no other choice. If you do choose this option, read the books that we have outlined above. But make sure that your child is being seen regularly by a mental health provider, so that if a problem arises a professional is at hand and ready to intervene.

In part 2 we have focused on helping you understand treatment and find providers that will suit your child's needs. Your child is about to embark on a course that will weaken the OCD bully. This work will be difficult. So what can you as a parent do to support this process? We will explore that subject in part 3.

Psychiatrist Interview

What are your hours? _____

Do you accept my insurance and how do you handle claim submission and payments? _____

What is you cost per session? How long does a session last? _____

How long are the initial assessment visits? _____

How many assessment visits are usually completed before medication is started? _____

How soon could we get an appointment? _____

What are the frequency and length of visits during early treatment?

_____

What are the frequency and length of visits after the patient is stabilized?

_____

Do you work with children with OCD? What medications do you usually prescribe? _____

Do you work with children who also have difficulties with (list any other problems of concern)? _____

Do you do psychotherapy for OCD? _____

    If so, what kind? _____

    If not, will you work with a psychologist of my choosing? _____

    Can you recommend any psychologists? _____

Personal impression of the psychiatrist: _____

Information from the License Board:

Is the psychiatrist's license in good standing? Have any disciplinary actions been taken against this clinician? _____

Chart 5a

Therapist Interview

What are your hours? _____

Do you accept my insurance and how do you handle claim submission and payments? _____

Cost and length of evaluation: _____

Cost and length of sessions: _____

How soon can we get an evaluation? _____

When can therapy start? _____

Will you be able to commit to weekly appointments at a standing time?
_____

Approximately how many children with OCD have you seen? How long have you done this kind of work? _____

What kind of treatment techniques do you use in their treatment?
_____

In the early phases of treatment, how often do you expect to see the child? (Visits should be approximately once a week unless the problem is very severe requiring more intensive work.) _____

When necessary, do you see children more than once per week? _____

When necessary, are you willing to make home visits and/or do you do work outside the office? _____

Do you work with schools? If so, what do you typically do? (Therapist should be willing to attend meetings and communicate with school personnel regularly.) _____

On average, how long does your typical treatment last? (Rule out this therapist if the answer sounds like forever.) _____

Do you work with children who also have difficulties with (list any other problems of concerns)? _____

Personal impressions of the therapist: _____

Information from the License Board:

Is the therapist's license in good standing? Have any disciplinary actions been taken against this clinician? _____

Chart 5b

Part III

What the Parent Can Do

In part 1, you learned all about OCD. In part 2, you learned all about treatment. You are ready to begin this journey with your child and you feel eager to start the work. But wait one moment. Living with OCD is about living with paradoxes, and a paradox is about to slap you in the face. Your natural desire is to take control, to solve the problem, to get your child back on track. The paradox is this: If you want to solve this problem and get it under control, then *don't.* You cannot solve this problem, because it is not your problem to solve. This is one of those times in parenting where the more you try to fix the problem, the worse you will make it. The more parents consider it their job to fix OCD, the harder the child works to protect and defend the OCD. If you care too much, your child will not care enough. There is only one driver's seat, and if you are in it then your child is just along for the ride.

So, if you're not the driver, then who are you and what can you do? In part 3, we'll help you define your role and your responsibilities. You'll learn how to develop more constructive attitudes and observe your child and your family so that you'll be prepared to be helpful when the need arises. We'll assist you in developing a plan to galvanize the entire family to support your child's efforts. We'll speak plainly about discipline and discuss your role in the school. Finally, we'll focus on your need to take care of yourself and on the fact that fighting OCD needs to be a lifestyle choice that carries into the future.

Chapter 6

Defining Roles and Responsibilities

Treating the child with OCD requires a team approach. There are many people on the child's team in this fight against the opponent, OCD. In this chapter we'll discuss the concept of working as a team and each team member's role. We'll then help you adapt these roles to meet the needs of individual children.

Ideally, in the game of fighting OCD, the therapist is the head coach, the child is the player, and the parents are assistant coaches. A parent acting as the head coach may work in Little League, but it will probably not serve you or your child well here. We discussed how to find a therapist in part 2. We are making the assumption that you have a therapist who is willing to play the role, however imperfectly, of head coach.

The Therapist's Role

In sports, children are brought to a coach to learn how to win games and defeat opponents. Likewise, children are brought to a therapist (head coach) to learn how to defeat their OCD. A good coach has a vision for the child's future that they are working toward. To be successful, the head coach must perform many responsibilities well:

◊   Maintain a vision of the child's future and encourage the child to work toward that future.

◊   Teach the player the rules and the plays of the game—what makes OCD stronger and what makes it weak so the right choice can be identified in any OC moment.

◊   Teach the player about the opponent—how to recognize the OCD.

◊   Design exercises to build strength and skill—use appropriate E/RP exercises.

◊   Convey other skills to support the plays—teach how and when to use other cognitive behavioral therapy (CBT) tools.

◊   Inspire the player—light a fire beneath the child to motivate him or her to fight hard.

◊   Pace the player—push without overwhelming the child.

◊   Express confidence in the player—bring out the child's inherent strengths.

◊   Keep proper focus—remind the child of long-term progress while staying focused on the present.

◊   Support the player after a loss—comfort and refocus the child.

◊   Manage, instruct, and coach the assistant coaches.

The Child's Role

What is the child's role in this process? As the player in the game, his or her role, first and foremost, is to find a desire and reason to win the game, and then use that reason to play the game. The player in this game has his or her own important responsibilities:

◊   Learn from the coach—attempt to understand what the coach teaches.

◊   Discuss problems—be open about difficulties, obstacles, or confusion.

◊   Be honest—tell the truth when doing therapy homework (for example, don't say that your temperature was a 3 if it was actually a 9) so that your coach can help you solve problems.

◊   Practice! Practice! Practice!—most of the learning takes place during practice.

◊ *Play the game*—make the right choice in any particular OCD moment.

◊ Be brave—risk failure and anxiety. Be willing to be challenged.

◊ Ask for support—decide when help is needed and communicate that need.

◊ Analyze losses—learn from mistakes and decide on different choices.

◊ Work hard—do extra practicing to get stronger in the areas in which you could improve.

◊ Be a good sport—be gentle with yourself when you lose, and focus on improving.

◊ Celebrate victories—take credit for successes, no matter how small.

◊ Focus on a winning season—work hard now, but remember it's a lengthy process and no single event determines the outcome.

The Parent's Role

The parent's role is to *be a parent first and an assistant coach second*. Most parents who feel out of control because of a child's OCD believe that normal parenting "doesn't work with my child" and that actually something else is necessary. Rather than operating first as the parent, they may have taken on some other primary role, such as schoolteacher (homeschooling); advocate (working to get special accommodations for the child at school or in some activity); or therapist. Assuming other roles sacrifices the parental role because as a result being the parent becomes somehow less important. Thus, many of the good parenting skills that parents demonstrate with their children who do not have OCD are left unused with their child who does. A major part of your supportive role will be to rediscover your useful parenting tools and use them again to parent your child with OCD.

Responsibilities of the Assistant Coach

In addition to the major task of rediscovering your parenting tools, you will need to act as an assistant coach in the therapy process. As assistant coach, you will have important responsibilities too.

Take Care of Yourself

The assistant coach needs to be ready to support the player throughout the whole process, which requires being strong and healthy and necessitates that you take care of yourself physically and emotionally.

Educate Yourself

The assistant coach needs to learn everything about the opponent and the process of playing the game. Understanding is important because you'll want to know, in any instance, what action will promote healthy functioning in the long run and how best to get your child to follow through. Additionally, understanding OCD will help you empathize with your child as he or she faces difficult tasks; model confidence in the process, the outcome, and your child's ability to persevere; recognize healthy actions in the midst of distress or failure; and provide accurate feedback and good advice to your child when problems occur at home.

Trust the Coach and the Process

One of the toughest jobs for the assistant coach is to trust the head coach and trust the process. This means showing up without your own agenda. The assistant coach must follow the plan created by the head coach and player. Departing from that plan can undermine the authority of the head coach, possibly weaken the relationship between the head coach and player, and jeopardize the supportive role of the assistant coach. If you have concerns about progress or your child's level of involvement, raise the issue privately with the therapist, who can then make judicious use of that information. Another facet of trusting the process is to stay focused on the current game. Dwelling on past losses or on upcoming challenges interferes with the player's ability to focus on the current problem. It's important to help your child stay focused on the *present*.

Motivate the Player

A major responsibility of the assistant coach is to motivate the player. When a player is challenged by OCD, the assistant coach can motivate by reminding the player why winning is important. If a child has no reason to win, then it's the responsibility of the assistant coach to create reasons or rewards that can motivate the child.

A critical aspect of maintaining motivation is remembering the journey. Children often forget where they started, looking at the current exposure exercises as more threatening than any of the previous ones. Remembering the starting point, and important victories along the way, can pump up a child's confidence so he or she can push on. To keep motivation high, it is necessary to celebrate and encourage every gain. To be effective, praise must match your child's style. Effusiveness will miss the mark with a low-key child, while just a nod will not do for a child who craves praise and attention.

Looking back and looking forward can both be helpful when it comes to appreciating your child's level of functioning. Parents tend to focus on all the things their children cannot do instead of what they can do. Sonya often felt overwhelmed by the seemingly endless task of cleaning her room, sorting through the piles of school papers, movie tickets, candy wrappers, and other paper items. Her parents also felt frustrated, but they were encouraged when they remembered that just a few months earlier, Sonya wouldn't consider giving up even one item. Now, she was discarding a few items every day, despite sometimes extreme anxiety.

Look back to the time when your child was first diagnosed. List things your child could not do then that he or she can do now. Also, list activities that he or she avoided then but does not avoid now. _____

_____

_____

_____

List your child's recent victories (even if they are only small moves forward).

_____

_____

_____

Revisit these questions at least once a month.

Prevent Burnout

Another very important role of the assistant coach is to prevent burnout. Fighting OCD is hard work that is made more difficult by fatigue, insufficient sleep, poor nutrition, sadness, low energy, or too much pressure. To be successful, a player must be fit—getting adequate food, rest, and fun.

Setting a priority means that in order to reach one goal you are willing to let other important tasks slide. To promote success, assistant coaches must make therapy and the process of fighting OCD the number one priority. Other things, such as music lessons and some household chores, become secondary; still others should be dropped. On the other hand, often the most important motivation to fight OCD is to win back some fun. Children whose only activity is fighting OCD can feel as burdened by therapy as by OCD. So when you set priorities, don't sacrifice all the fun.

For example, Sonya's parents realized their entire family was too busy. Everyone gave up some activities. Sonya continued with softball, but she took several weeks off from piano lessons.

Set Priorities

List all the activities your child is involved in. With your child, number them according to priority. In the space provided, write which activities can be dropped or reduced temporarily. Be sure to keep one fun activity near the top of the list.

1. _____

2. _____

3. _____

4. _____

5. _____

6. _____

7. _____

Oversee Practice

Some assistant coaches are responsible for overseeing practice at home, while others just need to be available. Generally, the head coach and player determine the level of participation that is needed. Whatever the decision, you'll need to stay out of the player's way and ask yourself, "How much help does my player *need*?" Only that much help should be offered *if* requested. Furthermore, the assistant coach does not have the freedom to push as hard as he or she or even the head coach might want. Assistant coaches should encourage but also let their players make their own choices.

Any avoidance or other problem that emerges during practice needs to be communicated to the head coach. Communicating this information is often best done either by e-mail or phone message before a session, since bringing these issues up verbally can derail the session. Verbal reporting also can seem intrusive to children and teens, who may lament that they feel policed and become uncooperative.

Know When to Get Out of the Way

The final responsibility of assistant coaches is to get out of the way when they cannot be helpful. Parents are unhelpful when they are angry and when they nag or police. Frustrated parents lash out, distracting children from their therapy challenges and providing them with new stresses. Conflict between team members damages the foundation of the treatment—that everyone is aligned against the OCD. Nagging and policing are also unhelpful because they erode the team spirit. E/RP exercises are not laws to be enforced; they are recommendations, instructions, and practices that the child *chooses* to do because of a desire to defeat OCD. When parents nag and police, they are taking too much responsibility.

Age-Appropriate Coaching

The responsibilities of the assistant coach listed above pretty much cover all assistant coaches. Now we'll begin to adjust your role to fit your individual child. We will describe four levels of assistant coaching that fall on a continuum from very involved (level I) to hardly involved (level IV). The kind of assistant coach you aspire to be should be loosely based on your child's age or maturity. Sometimes, severe symptoms or other issues (motivation, depression, personality issues) may necessitate your becoming more involved than the child's age would ordinarily suggest. When this occurs, just keep in mind the level of coaching that these guidelines suggest for you and work gradually with your child's therapist to get there.

Level I: Hands-On Assistant Coach for Young Children

For young children age six or seven, you will aspire to be a level I (L-I) assistant coach, virtually a second head coach. The L-I assistant coach should be present at every therapy session to ensure full understanding of the therapy by the child. Children this young can misunderstand the metaphors and concepts of therapy. Your presence allows you to clarify issues if confusion becomes evident at home. For example, many young children struggle with the concept of a "fear temperature." The L-I assistant coach may help between sessions by pointing out examples of increments seen in daily life: sizes that are small, medium, and large or temperatures that are cold, medium, and hot.

L-I assistant coaches are very active during practice at home. Expect to work with the therapist to come up with ways to make exposure fun for your child. Expect to help your child "spy on the OCD" (i.e., notice and record triggers for obsessions and rituals). Be willing to do any exposure exercise asked of your child. Also be prepared to reward your child frequently with small trinkets. Two principles are important in OCD treatment of children in this age group: (1) The process must be fun, and (2) for most young children, the more the enthusiasm generated by every gain, the better!

Level II: Assistant Coach for Children

Children ages eight to ten require a level II (L-II) assistant coach. L-II assistant coaches generally check in at the close of each therapy session. Check-ins apprise the L-II assistant coach of current work and weekly homework expectations, allowing opportunities for praise and discussions about rewards. The head coach and child inform the parent of any help the child would like during the week in order to complete their homework assignment. Frequently L-II assistant coaches need to help their players spy on the OCD.

L-II assistant coaches are sometimes present for every therapy session. Children in this age range usually grasp the concepts, metaphors, and analogies used in treatment quite well so they don't necessarily need their parents to be present to promote understanding, although some children will prefer their parents to attend every session. L-II assistant coaches need to follow the child's lead on this point. The presence of the L-II assistant coach in each session can improve the process because therapy concepts are more likely to permeate family culture. And having an additional person makes it easier to design fun therapeutic exposure games during the session. However, if parents are present at each session, the risk of the parent routinely speaking for the child increases, and it becomes more likely that the child will lose ownership of the process.

Level III: Flexible Assistant Coach for "Tweens"

Level III (L-III) assistant coaches for children ages eleven to thirteen must be flexible. Children of this age vacillate between wanting to be independent and wanting to be taken care of. The important principle guiding the L-III assistant coach is to maintain flexibility and not personalize the child's mixed messages. Your goal is to be helpful; sometimes this will mean being close by and active, and other times it will require stepping back and letting go. Let the child determine the extent of the L-III assistant coach's involvement and don't expect consistency.

Matching the child's needs to the amount and wording of praise becomes more important for the L-III assistant coaches. Making exposure exercises fun sometimes becomes less important for children this age, but it usually remains paramount. Again, the rule is to follow your child's lead. You can suggest a game or art activity, but don't insist.

Level IV: Hands-Off Assistant Coach for Teens

The rule of thumb for the level IV (L-IV) assistant coach for adolescents is to be as scarce as possible without being uninvolved. The developmental task of adolescence is to form identity and establish independence. These are the years when children need to break away from parents and establish confidence in their ability to think and act for themselves. This process necessarily entails rejecting you at least some of the time; rejecting parents creates space for the teen to figure out what he or she thinks and who he or she wants to be. In general, when a L-IV assistant coach becomes too involved, the child becomes less involved. So let your child and the therapist determine the course of therapy and how you can be most helpful. Respecting your child's wishes regarding therapy will benefit him or her, because it is important to encourage independence and personal responsibility at this age.

However, know what your boundaries are and be clear with your child and the therapist regarding what your limits are and what will necessitate your taking parental action. For example, sometimes a teen who is asserting independence also consistently makes poor decisions that strengthen the OCD. A L-IV assistant coach may feel a pull to become more involved, even to the point of sitting in on sessions and participating in homework exercises like a L-I assistant coach. A better option would be to maintain your role as an L-IV assistant coach but become a more involved parent. You may need to set limits around behaviors that affect the family or that jeopardize the physical well-being of your child. We will discuss parenting issues more in later chapters.

Some teens want more involved assistant coaches, expecting their parents to be present at every therapy session, to push them to do their exercises, and to participate in each exposure. These teens may be overly close to and dependent on one or both parents. They may hesitate to make any decisions independently and fear disappointing their parents. They may still reject their parents, but they hold on tight at the same time. Such children may require a L-I assistant coach to start, but parent and therapist need to work to help the parent achieve a more appropriate level of coaching for this age group.

Being an assistant coach will challenge you. It will utilize and stretch your parenting skills. The next chapter will help you prepare for this position on your child's team.

Chapter 7

Preparing to Be an Assistant Coach

Coaching your child in his or her struggle against OCD is a difficult job. The endeavor requires a bit of preparation. Your success will depend upon training yourself to think and do what works. You'll need to examine your own behavior for helpfulness and effectiveness. You'll need to focus on your goals and be willing to be flexible and creative in order to help your child get where he or she wants to go.

Grieve Your Loss

The first important task is to be honest with yourself about what you are feeling. Parents can harbor many feelings toward the OCD, toward their child who has the OCD, and toward the world in general because the situation exists. Many are angry, sad, depressed, and worried sick for their child. Often, parents feel guilty for having these feelings and pretend they don't exist. If you have these feelings, and you probably do, they can seriously diminish your usefulness as an assistant coach.

What exactly is the liability of having these negative feelings? When you are stuck with these feelings, you are more likely to become hostile or unsupportive, engaging in blaming or coercive activities. You may be worrying your child and causing your child to feel guilty for having this problem. But the biggest danger from these feelings results from pretending they aren't there, because they fester in silence. We aren't saying that you have to tell the world all about your child or your feelings about your child's struggle. We are saying that if you are not willing to admit to having these feelings, even to yourself, then it becomes much harder to let them go and get down to the business of being an assistant coach.

The truth of the matter is that discovering that your child has OCD is a significant loss for most parents. That loss requires grieving: anger, sadness, and tears. Don't shy away from feeling these emotions. You need to put your feelings into words so you can process what is happening. By allowing yourself to grieve the loss and integrating these feelings into your reality, you'll be in a better position to develop perspective on the problem.

Feeling angry about the injustice of your child having this disorder can cause you to get stuck comparing your life, and your child's life, to the life you had envisioned for your child and your family. The problem with such a comparison is that the life you had envisioned, which you are comparing to your reality, is a fantasy. Fantasies are always better than reality. So, you are really comparing apples with oranges. And, if your child did not have this problem, there would undoubtedly be some other problem for you to grapple with. Very few people lead charmed lives; OCD just happens to be the problem that your child has been dealt.

Gary's father, for example, reacted with anger and frustration to his son's checking compulsions and emotional outbursts. His mother responded by worrying about Gary's progress in school and assisting him in his checking, just to help him feel "okay." Both wondered why their child had to have such a "horrible," debilitating illness. But when a friend's child was diagnosed with a terminal illness and a niece was arrested for drug possession, both parents were able to see Gary's OCD from a different perspective.

Make seven copies of this worksheet and complete one each day for one week. Below, write about your feelings and thoughts regarding your child's struggle with OCD. Don't worry about justifying your feelings and thoughts, just write them down. They are not right or wrong.

This is an exposure exercise, much like the exposure exercises for the treatment of OCD. In this case, you are exposing yourself to the feelings of grief and sadness you have about your child's OCD. Doing this daily for a week will help you understand what a diagnosis of OCD means to you emotionally. Spending time with your feelings and thoughts will also help you find perspective.

_____

_____

_____

_____

_____

_____

_____

_____

_____

_____

_____

_____

_____

_____

Find Perspective

You probably don't like thinking or writing these thoughts because they are painful. Are you noticing that some particularly difficult ideas keep appearing? After you've completed this exercise every day for a week, list the recurring negative thoughts on a separate piece of paper and look at them. Are these as far as the thoughts go, or do some of the thoughts really hurt because they go further and mean something more to you? For each statement, ask yourself: Is this as painful as this one gets? Or does this mean something more to me? Is there some significance I give this thought that makes it even worse?

Once you have the thoughts boiled down to their most essential, painful kernel, you will be in a position to begin developing perspective. Most people do not have the time or energy to think through or analyze every situation in life in a balanced and realistic way. Instead, people often rely on thinking shortcuts to help them make sense of a situation. Taking shortcuts can be helpful because it allows a person to respond quickly and in the moment. However, sometimes relying on these shortcuts can cause a person to view a situation in an overly negative way and that can result in their feeling prolonged distress or reacting in a way that makes the problem worse. So when a situation or idea is particularly painful, it is often a good idea to revisit the issue and think it through more slowly in a deliberate and objective way.

The first step in finding perspective is to identify what kind of a thinking shortcut you may be taking. Five types of shortcuts are especially common and potentially harmful. The chances are that each of your bothersome thoughts will fall into at least one of these categories:

1. **Fortune-telling and catastrophizing:** thinking you know the future; perhaps anticipating your child will wind up homeless on some street or too fearful to leave his or her room or your house

2. **Mind reading:** thinking you know what others are thinking; believing that others are thinking horrible things about you or your child

3. **Overgeneralizing:** making patterns from incomplete information; believing that other parents and other children don't struggle

4. **Labeling:** calling yourself or your child names or putting yourselves in negative categories; thinking your child is crazy or thinking of yourself as weak

5. **Emotional reasoning:** letting your emotions do all of your thinking

Make many copies of the blank Negative Thoughts Chart that follows so that you will have extras on hand whenever you might need them. Now list those most painful thoughts you have just identified on a copy of the Negative Thoughts Chart. Because these thoughts represent your core problematic beliefs, you will probably find that many of your original thoughts keep coming down to the same idea, and your list will be shorter than it was before. These are the beliefs that are causing you the most heartache now and can potentially interfere with your becoming an effective assistant coach. Review the thinking shortcuts explained above and identify for each problematic thought the category of shortcut that you may be taking.

Each day, work on thinking through one of your listed thoughts. On a separate piece of paper answer the questions listed below for that category. After answering, do you still believe the painful thought as strongly? Or is it possible to shift your perspective in such a way that the realistic part of your concern is not denied, while the issue is generally less painful and easier to cope with? If so, write down a more objective statement on your Negative Thoughts Chart. Continue this exercise daily until you have addressed all of your problematic beliefs.

1. Fortune-telling and catastrophizing

◊ What evidence is there that this event will happen?

◊ Is there any evidence that this event won't happen?

◊ Are there other events that could realistically happen instead?

◊ What does getting stuck on this idea do to my ability to function as a supportive assistant coach? Does it help or hinder me? Would an alternative perspective work better?

2. Mind reading

◊ What evidence do I have that people will think or react in the way I am anticipating?

◊ Is there any evidence that people will think or react in some other way?

◊ Am I only worrying about what some people will think, and ignoring the opinions of other, relevant people who may be more compassionate, understanding, or knowledgeable? Should the opinions of these other people count as well?

◊ What does getting stuck on this idea do to my ability to function as a supportive assistant coach? Does it help or hinder me? Would an alternative perspective work better?

3. Overgeneralizing

◊ Am I thinking in black and white only? What are the gray zones that I might be neglecting?

◊ Am I forgetting exceptions to the generalities?

◊ Would people I admire or respect look at this situation in this way, or would they look at it in some other way?

◊ What does getting stuck on this idea do to my ability to function as a supportive assistant coach? Does it help or hinder me? Would an alternative perspective work better?

4. Labeling

◊ In my more compassionate moments, what do I think about this name that I am calling my child or myself?

◊ What would I think about someone else using this label?

◊ Is it possible that using this label riles me up in an overly emotional state?

◊ What does using this language do to my ability to function as a supportive assistant coach? Does it help or hinder me? Would adopting other words work better?

5. Emotional reasoning

◊ What are my feelings telling me and what is the evidence telling me? Are the two in agreement?

◊ If there are no facts supporting my feelings, does it make sense to believe my feelings outright?

◊ What makes me think that my gut is always right? Has this habit of trusting and going with my feelings despite what my head is saying caused me problems in the past?

◊ What does my believing this feeling to be the truth do to my ability to function as a supportive assistant coach? Does it help or hinder me? What is an alternative way of viewing this that acknowledges my feelings but also allows room for the facts?

Protect Your Resources

In order to maintain your equilibrium while being an assistant coach, you will need to protect and nourish your own resources—you cannot afford to attend to everyone else and not take care of yourself. We will devote more attention to this issue in chapter 11, but in order to prepare yourself now, you need to do at least the bare minimum to ensure you are taking care of yourself. You and your child need adequate nutrition, exercise, rest, and fun. You need to devote time every day to replenishing yourself, whether that means finding emotional or spiritual support, meditating, listening to calm music, or taking a walk. Ideally, you will carve out time for all these activities regularly. This will not always seem possible. If there never seems to be time for you, then you probably need to either rethink your priorities or find some creative means of delegation. Your needs shouldn't be routinely sacrificed.

Negative Thoughts Chart

Negative Thought	Category	Objective Statement

Chart 7a

List all the activities you are involved in. Include work, school, church activities, volunteer work, your children's extracurricular activities, therapy, self-care, and leisure activities. (You do participate in *some* leisure activities, don't you?) Number them according to priority. Make sure that at least one self-care or leisure activity falls somewhere in the top seven. If you can't, do what you can to delegate responsibilities or rearrange your activities. Make room for yourself in your life.

1. _____

2. _____

3. _____

4. _____

5. _____

6. _____

7. _____

8. _____

9. _____

10. _____

11. _____

12. _____

Adopt the Right Attitudes

Your success as an assistant coach will largely hinge on your ability to master and model new attitudes for your child. You will need to change in order to provide the right example and emotional environment for your child. The parental attitudes that contribute to a child's success in learning to live with OCD do not seem like typical parenting philosophies. Actually, they can be useful to any parent who is struggling with a child's behavior problem. It will be difficult for your child to accept, master, and adopt these attitudes. He or she will need to see them in action to be able to take them on for himself or herself. Thus, the change has to begin with you. You need to adopt these seemingly foreign attitudes in order to become a truly effective assistant coach.

Embrace Uncertainty

"What if I lose my job?" "What if I have an accident?" "What if my children get sick?" These kinds of thoughts are universal experiences. Most people do not find these "what ifs?" tormenting because they are able to shift their focus to what is occurring in the present. They delay considering future possible problems until the possibilities have in fact become realities in the present. These people are living their lives with uncertainty, tolerating the possibility of horrific events on a daily basis without attempting to control the future by avoiding every possible catastrophe. However, "what if?" thoughts feel like a flash of ESP to the person with OCD. He or she thinks, "I thought this, so that must mean it's going to happen." The person with OCD feels he or she must prevent the inevitable. What people with OCD really believe is, "Life is unthinkable and unacceptable with this possibility in it. I would not be able or willing to go on if this thing happened."

When looked at this way, each effort to control the future and gain certainty can be seen as an act of mistaken self-importance—the act of a puny human being shaking a fist at the universe and saying, "No! Life will be unacceptable if *that* happens." Unfortunately, this attitude denies reality. Ultimately, we each have control over only a very small part of our lives. Hence, we can take comfort from the Reinhold Niebuhr quote, made famous by Alcoholics Anonymous, "God grant me the serenity to accept things I cannot change, the courage to change things I can, and wisdom to know the difference." As human beings, we don't get to choose what life will give us, and to attempt to assume such control is, at best, a losing battle.

So, what does this have to do with becoming an assistant coach? The child's need for certainty can be contagious. Parents, picking up their child's anxiety, wonder, "What if my child doesn't get better?" "When will my child get better?" "What if the medication isn't right?" "What if he doesn't go along with the treatment?" "What if I say or do the wrong thing?" "What if she can't go to college?" Parents, out of love for their children, want to make every move without any mistakes. They want guarantees that bad things won't happen to their children. Unfortunately, we don't get to choose the lives that our children are dealt and we don't get to live those lives for them. We do not have control. Even they do not have full control. There are just too many possibilities outside of anyone's control.

What is open to you, what you *can* control, is to model an attitude that will help you and your child—an attitude of "embracing uncertainty." In other words, say yes to life with all of its negative possibilities. Embracing uncertainty means being willing to say, "Life is acceptable *no matter what,* with all of its negative possibilities." It means being willing to stand with our children with optimism, even when their lives are hit by such things as OCD, and even when the OCD clamors that people might die or other disasters might occur in the absence of the rituals. We may not know exactly how everything is going to turn out, and we may not make every right decision along the way, but when we embrace uncertainty we make the best decisions we can and do not quit if we fall down. "Embracing uncertainty" means believing that life is good and can be good even though we don't have full control, and even if unthinkably bad things can happen. It means accepting ourselves with all our imperfections and accepting others with all their imperfections. Mostly, embracing uncertainty means living in the moment and appreciating the gifts we have, without trying to safeguard tomorrow's tomorrow.

When assistant coaches try to embrace uncertainty, they are much more able to weather the ups and downs of their child's disorder and to find the humor in life. They're more able to savor the special gifts their children have to offer and to take risks when they're not certain of the best approach. Most important, they're free to live in each moment, making the best decision that they can, using the information at their disposal. Embracing uncertainty is the attitude that we want our children with OCD to master. This is the attitude that lets them say yes to life.

Gary felt a need for absolute certainty about the answers he gave on tests and homework papers. He had to be certain his backpack was in order, too. When he was worried and emotional, his mother also became worried. Each day's homework assignment seemed extremely important. As a family, they learned to accept and even embrace uncertainty, asking, "What's the worst that could happen? Maybe Gary will flunk fourth grade for forgetting his math book!" Then they'd laugh at the absurdity and say, "Okay, we'll deal with that if it happens!"

Let Go of "Normal"

Almost all children and adults with OCD who seek treatment dream of being "normal." They want to be like everyone else. Parents also harbor this same dream and expectation. However, there are many problems that go along with this deep craving of parents and children alike. First, be careful what you wish for. Remember that the majority of children with this disorder are extremely bright, precocious, imaginative, creative, thoughtful, and loving. For most, the OCD is clearly the downside to all of their very positive qualities. If you could, would you really trade in all of these qualities for a "normal" child?

Second, this craving for normal is a huge obstacle to your child's progress in therapy and your ability to function as an assistant coach. When normal is the goal, most people want to restrict their activities to do "normal stuff"—they want to reject the "non-normal" therapy exercises. The first problem with this is that without extreme exercises, functioning will probably never approach the normal range. It is the extreme exercises that weaken the OCD most effectively. Therefore, your clinging to normal encourages your child to cling to normal and ultimately limits your coaching effectiveness.

Another problem, pointed out by Dr. Jon Grayson in his talks, is that you and your child can't adequately assess what's normal. The only way that anyone can guess what's normal is by asking others without OCD what they do. This assumes that they *know* what they do. Most people are lousy reporters of their own functioning. In addition, if asked, for example, under what circumstances they wash their hands, people often lie. They don't lie deliberately or maliciously; they answer by saying what they try to do, rather than what they actually do. In other words, they will tell you the socially desirable response because that is what they, in good conscience, try to do.

But the truth of the matter is that people only follow social conventions when it is convenient and not too much trouble to do so. They vary in their performance of these tasks. This is exactly how they differ from people with OCD, who are highly consistent in the attention they bestow on these activities. People without OCD don't pay attention and they get these things wrong all the time (hence the signs in public rest rooms reminding people to wash their hands). So while "normal" people report that they lock their door at night, lock their car, wash their hands after using the bathroom, and wash their hands before eating, they don't tell you about all the times they forget. They don't tell you about those times they might have forgotten to do these things because, to them, those times are exceptions and don't count because they are not in line with their intended behavior.

Another problem with craving "normality" is that once your child has made progress, he or she will want to be considered "fixed" or "cured." Therefore, he or she will resist adopting a lifestyle that includes regular relapse-prevention exercises. As a result, he or she will be much more vulnerable to relapse. As an assistant coach, you can espouse the idea that "normality," if it even exists in the first place, is not all it's cracked up to be, and it certainly isn't something to aspire to. Let go of that dream. The truth is that people with OCD are not normal: they are often brighter, more creative, more imaginative, and more morally inclined than the average person. They are also more vulnerable to their own anxieties and fears, even when they are managing their OCD. As a result, they need to take a different path in life. Parents who accept this reality will make it easier for their children to accept it, by just taking these truths in stride.

Dr. Fitzgibbons is often asked, "Isn't it possible that my child will outgrow this?" We don't know how many children outgrow their OCD because few studies have been done on this subject, and because OCD has really only recently been recognized in children. To best help your child, err on the safe side, preparing him or her to embrace a lifestyle that promotes self-acceptance and acknowledges being "different." Becoming an assistant coach necessitates letting go of the fantasy of your child being "normal," "cured," or "fixed." Instead, build a realistic vision of the future, a vision of your adult child living a productive and satisfying life, complete with work, family, and fun, managing OCD so effectively that it has minimal importance in his or her life.

Understand Anxiety

A critical hurdle for children with OCD and for their parents is to shift their thinking about anxiety and change their responses to it. This change can begin with you. Humans are wired to feel anxiety and fear to help us sense and keep ourselves out of danger. Functional anxiety in anticipation of some event or danger can prompt a person to take potentially lifesaving precautions. Functional fear is elicited by clear danger and can lead to a lifesaving escape or defense. So, fear and anxiety have been our friends throughout humanity's history, helping to ensure survival.

These emotions don't function properly in someone with an anxiety disorder such as OCD. The anxiety is triggered too easily, resulting in excessive and time-consuming planning, problem solving, and preventive actions even when the likelihood of real threat is low. Furthermore, fear is elicited as if there were real danger present, when in fact there is no threat to safety at all. Because of both the frequency and the intensity of the anxious or fearful response, the emotions lose their adaptive benefit and interfere with functioning. Over time, both the person suffering the intense emotions and those observing that person come to think of these emotions as negative instead of useful. For most people with an anxiety disorder, whether adults or children, anxiety does not feel "functional"; rather, it feels like a big bugaboo.

There are two prongs to every fear in every anxiety disorder. The first prong of the fear is the specific thing the person fears: spiders, dogs, flying, death, germs, accidents, being incomplete, feeling unsure, or not being right. The second prong is the thoughts the person has with regard to the fear: "I will feel anxious. I will feel that utterly horrible feeling and I won't be able to handle it." "The feeling may spiral out of control." "I might break into a zillion pieces." "It might go on forever, or make me crazy, or make me look foolish. It will feel intolerable."

The second prong of the fear is as powerful a factor in motivating avoidance and maintaining the fear as the first prong. If someone thinks that something is going to feel horrible, regardless of the actual threat, he or she won't want to do it. The most natural course of action is to avoid it. Therefore, the fear of the fear itself motivates avoidance and strengthens the fear in all anxiety disorders.

What happens to you, the parent, in this process? Over time, you too learn to be afraid of your child's anxiety. You know that if your child has to encounter what he or she is afraid of, then an upset will soon follow—your child may become frozen or have a tantrum. Soon, you start to think of anxiety as bad. A successful day comes to equal a day with little anxiety and no "meltdowns." A successful day becomes one where you've avoided all the hidden mines. Inadvertently, you begin to find ways to circumvent the anxiety in order to help your child get through the day. In essence, you enter into cahoots with your child's anxiety and end up working in the service of the anxiety. Successful avoidance then strengthens the idea that anxiety and fear are bad.

Over time, this attitude can develop into a desire to protect your child from any stress because OCD experiences do tend to worsen at times of stress. As this tendency becomes entrenched, a negative cycle is established where challenges are too frightening and stressful to be attempted, and self-esteem and confidence are eroded as challenges are avoided. Additionally, failures and mistakes become dreaded outcomes rather than opportunities for learning. Obviously, this cycle can be very harmful and damaging. The longer the cycle continues, the harder it is to turn it around.

See Anxiety as a Potential Friend

You can stop the cycle by working to change how you both think about anxiety. While it's true that the anxiety of OCD feels unpleasant, it's not dangerous. Even on the worst days, when your child has endless meltdowns, it's not dangerous. The only real danger from anxiety comes from how one deals with it. Children who act out aggressively toward others or themselves can be dangerous. But it's not the anxiety that's dangerous; it's the child's choice to react with aggression that's potentially dangerous.

The only time when anxiety itself may be dangerous is when the child or adult has a history of psychosis. In such cases, extremely high anxiety could contribute to a psychotic break. It's very rare for children with OCD to struggle with psychosis. While the concerns of a child with OCD may seem crazy to both the parent and the child, the child is rarely psychotic. In fact, the child's concern that his or her worries might be crazy is in itself very strong evidence that he or she is quite sane. Thus, the possibility of anxiety being dangerous for your child is very low.

Anxiety can and should be your friend. The sooner you can shift your thinking, the better. Anxiety is your friend because it is a willingness to embrace the anxiety that will defy the OCD. Making peace with every fear requires saying okay to the anxiety and opening oneself to it. Children (and adults) frequently believe that a successful exposure is one in which you do the exercise and you feel fine. While such an experience is great, doing an exposure and not feeling the fear is typically the reward you get *after* you have repeatedly done the same exposure and felt the anxiety and fear many times. You say, "Okay, give it to me." "Hit me with your best shot." "Pitch me your worst." When people do that, first they feel "bad" or anxious, and then they slowly begin to feel better as the fear loses its power.

Think of anxiety as an ice cube. When you pick it up in your hands, it hurts, but as you hold it and it melts, it loses its ability to cause the same kind of pain it first caused. The more you touch the melted water the warmer and less unpleasant it becomes. You don't need to anticipate pain from that ice cube ever again, unless of course you choose to "avoid" it by putting it back in the freezer. Yes, anxiety can be painful, but it is also transforming. When you accept the discomfort that precedes transformation, you receive the gift of peace.

Anxiety is also your friend and your child's friend as it pops up throughout the day. Why? Because anxiety is like a big neon sign that flashes "Opportunity." Before therapy, your child felt that the big flashing sign read "Run Away." In truth, however, every situation that triggers anxiety affords an opportunity for children with OCD to learn they can fight back. Rather than run away, they can say yes to their fear, pick it up, and transform it. By doing so, they win another battle and take another step toward getting back their life.

Finally, anxiety is your friend and your child's friend because when the OCD is running in low gear in the background rather than the foreground, functional anxiety and functional fear begin to surface. As we have already mentioned, these emotions exist for a purpose. Not only do they help us survive but they actually sharpen our ability to lead productive lives. All challenges bring anxiety and stress. To function at our best, we need these emotions. To view these emotions as functional and important means that your child is free to respond appropriately to the anxiety and fear they feel in frightening or danger-ous situations. They will no longer feel crippled and unable to respond appropriately to real threat cues because of frantic responding to false alarms.

When children view anxiety as a friend, as a transforming emotion, and as a signal of opportunity, an interesting thing happens. Rather than running away, they will be more likely to approach. They will begin to take pride in their courage. Rather than spending time doing rituals, they will be free to live their lives. When you view anxiety this way, you make it easier for your child to grasp the concept. In addition, your take on a day of twenty meltdowns changes to seeing it as a day that was full of opportunity and probably courageous effort with some victories, rather than as an experience that you don't want to do again.

When you view anxiety as a transformative friend, you no longer have to foresee and protect your child from every pitfall. Rather, when you see a potentially anxiety-laden situation on the horizon you can concentrate on encouraging your child to meet the challenge. If the child avoids it, you can wistfully remark that there will be other opportu-nities to accept the challenge and that all is not lost. (This response is much more effective than communicating that it was a narrow escape and how wonderful it is that he or she didn't "lose it.") Over time, your child learns that you have faith in his or her resilience and ability to cope. Your child also learns that you value most the willingness to meet challenges and take risks, rather than valuing only success. As a result, your child's self-esteem becomes stronger.

Gary's mother dreaded the nights before big tests. She knew her son would be anxious and worried. With therapy, the anxiety, frustration, and checking were reduced but not eliminated. Often, he felt angry with himself for getting worked up over a test or homework assignment. Gary's father, once the one to get angry, helped the family recog-nize these nights as opportunities to challenge the OCD. The real "test" wasn't the next day, in school, but there at home, facing the OCD.

Keep track of every negative thought you have or comment you make about your child's anxiety or distress for two days. For each thought or comment, identify the situa-tion that triggered your child's discomfort and your thought. Once you have multiple examples, reframe the scenarios. Identify the "opportunities" hidden in the situations; find the silver lining in the discomfort. Write other comments that you can tell yourself and use to encourage your child that will both empathize with your child's distress and communi-cate your willingness to be friends with the anxiety.

Making Anxiety Your Friend

Negative thought or comment about child's distress	Situation that triggered child's distress	Alternative, encouraging thought or comment about child's distress

Chart 7b

Many parents believe that the foundation of self-esteem is a bank of success experiences. While these experiences do contribute to self-esteem by helping children feel good about their abilities and skills, there is another equally important building block. This other building block is the children's understanding that they can 'fall down, fail, make mistakes, and get back up. It's through these experiences that children learn they have what it takes to learn from their mistakes, and that mistakes and failures are not necessarily bigger than they are.

This chapter has helped to prepare you for the challenge of supporting your child as an assistant coach. Despite the fact that you may now be more personally prepared to begin, you are not yet fully equipped. The next chapter will continue the process of preparation by helping you to observe yourself, your child, and your family so that you will have the information you need to form and implement a plan.

Chapter 8

Observing How OCD Affects Your Family

When devising a game plan, the first thing to do is observe the situation. People tend to be lousy observers of behavior, so your first task is to improve your powers of observation. We'll help you learn to observe effectively and gather information that will be helpful to both your therapist and yourself in the fight against OCD. These observations will include the entire family, focusing on your affected child, yourself, and other family members.

"Spy on the Bully": Observe OCD Symptoms

Parents know their children better than anyone, and they have a greater opportunity to observe OCD symptoms than anyone else, except perhaps the child's teachers. Your ability to observe your child can be a tremendous asset to anyone attempting to help. This doesn't mean you'll need to follow your child around to spy on every behavior or interrogate your child like the OC police. Your child may welcome your help in making observations later in therapy when he or she is learning to spy on the OCD bully, but for now take it slow and concentrate on quietly paying attention to and tracking what is readily apparent to you.

We have designed two worksheets to help you begin improving your observations and collecting useful data. Begin by observing and keeping a log of rituals you notice and the stimuli that seem to prompt those behaviors, using the Observing OCD Behavior chart. This chart also provides room for you to note what your child avoids. Be sure to include rituals or avoidance foisted on you and other family members by your child, for example endless questions to you about safety or instructions not to wash their clothes with other people's laundry. Finally, use this form to note any products that your child uses excessively (extra shampoo, extra toilet paper, food waste, etc.). On the second form, Problems (Observed or Complained of) During the Day, note problems that your child experiences each day and attempt to determine whether these problems are related to the OCD. Track these things as well as you can, indicating those that you are sure of and those that you are less clear about.

Additionally, pay attention to your child's moods and rate anxiety, depression, and anger on a ten-point scale daily, with 10 being the "worst ever." This is an important exercise, because parents generally view their child as "okay" or "not okay." The ratings are meant to provide you with a rudimentary yardstick with which to compare relative experiences, so that over time you will be able to appreciate subtle changes. For all of the ratings, 1 should mean that everything is fine. For depression, 10 would mean that your child is talking about suicide and looks very depressed throughout the day. For anxiety, 10 would mean that your child is experiencing frequent full-blown panic attacks (in which the anxiety is so intense that he or she can hardly breathe and fears dying or losing control just from the panic). For anger, 10 would mean that your child is losing physical control and assaulting people or breaking things multiple times during the day.

We recommend that you make many copies of the blank Observing OCD Behavior worksheet and the Problems (Observed or Complained of) During the Day worksheet, fill them out daily, and keep them in a loose-leaf binder. Begin this observation process at least one week before your assessment interview with the therapist and bring the completed pages with you. Completing these worksheets throughout the course of therapy and sharing them with your child's therapist will keep him or her informed of progress or the lack thereof. It will also help you appreciate your child's progress when you feel frustrated because changes seem to occur too slowly.

Observing OCD Behavior

Date:

Stimulus/ Activity	Rituals (Indicate whether by child or family member.)	Approximate repetitions		Approximate time		OC logic to ritual (What the bully is saying—Indicate whether known from child or your hunch.)	Observed distress (1–10)
		Per episode	Per day	Per episode	Per day		

Observed avoidance (Indicate who must do it, child or family member.)			
Stimulus/ Activity	Avoidance behavior		

Excessive substance usage (e.g., shampoo, toilet paper, food)	Reason for excessive consumption

Chart 8a

Problems (Observed or Complained of) During the Day

Date:

Problem	How is it related to OCD? (Indicate if connection endorsed by child.)

Today's successes

Daily Ratings

Rate (1–10)			Sleep		Rate (good, fair, or poor) to indicate symptom interference		
Anxiety	Depression	Anger	Hours in bed	Hours asleep	Appetite	Activity	School/ Homework

Current medications and dosages:

Chart 8b

Observe Your Own Negative Behavior

An important aspect of supporting your child will be to refrain from contributing hostility and turmoil to your child's problems. You will not change your child by nagging, yelling, policing, persuading, or humiliating. We cannot emphasize enough how harmful these activities can be. These actions can demoralize your child almost as much as the OCD itself. Your task is always to encourage your child, to look for successes, and to provide praise for whatever courage is mustered. Put simply, all anger on your part must stop. Because ceasing this kind of behavior is so important, we suggest that you begin to attempt to change it *immediately* (rather than waiting until chapter 9, when you'll develop a family plan). This is a very tall order because most of these negative behaviors are the result of your desperation. But therapy provides the possibility of change, and you must put your faith in this process.

Parents may respond to this advice by saying, "I can sometimes keep my cool with the rituals, but how should I handle the disrespectful behavior that my child engages in?" Oftentimes, the rude behavior of children with OCD is a distracter. In essence, when a child with OCD riles a parent up by acting in a disrespectful or otherwise unacceptable way, the parent becomes distracted by this behavior, and the child gets let off the hook for the OCD-related task he or she wanted to avoid. Furthermore, if the parent loses it, the child often discovers that the accompanying parental guilt results in the parent backing off. We don't mean that children with OCD are *intentionally* manipulative. All children learn to do what works, and if getting parents riled up works to get them off some unwanted hook, then that's what they do.

It's important to control your frustration and anger because you need to keep the OCD in the forefront. Nearly everything else should take a backseat to the fight against OCD. We recommend that you learn to accept hostility calmly, while keeping your priorities in focus. When your child is angry, say, "You may think I'm horrible, but I'm not going to continue to feed your OCD by doing what we have agreed to stop." Maintaining this supportive attitude will be easier if you don't personalize your child's hostile verbiage; think of it as meaningless noise.

Rodney insisted that no chemicals be used in the house. Because of his fear that chemicals from outside might be brought into the house, he demanded that family members remove their shoes in the garage and change clothes as soon as they got home. The family worked together to develop a plan to gradually stop avoiding chemicals and changing shoes and clothing. Despite the fact that Rodney was instrumental in choosing the weekly goals, each week when the time came to make changes he often became angry, shouting obscenities at his parents. Instead of responding with anger, Rodney's parents acknowledged how difficult it must be for him to make the changes but reminded him that they were all dedicated to helping him fight the OCD.

Your task is to cease hostile behavior. This injunction is equivalent to the dictate to abstain from rituals that your child will receive. While blowing off steam provides you temporary relief, such venting erodes the healing process. When you practice facing your

Parent's Negative Behavior Monitoring Form

Date:

Child's negative behavior	Parent's negative behavior (Check all that apply.)						Parent's possible alternative behavior
	Nagging	Yelling	Persuading	Hostile looks	Snide comments	Laughing/ Joking at child	
Parent's negative behaviors totals							

Chart 8c

child's hostility without returning fire, you will find that the urge to lose it becomes less intense. To help you we have created the Parent's Negative Behavior Monitoring Form for you to use to track your negative behaviors. Monitoring, which increases awareness, is one of behavior therapy's most effective tools for helping to change any behavior, because you can't change a behavior unless you are aware of it. For maximum effectiveness, carry a worksheet with you at all times so that you can record a negative behavior immediately after engaging in one. Record your child's negative behavior in the left column. Indicate your negative behaviors with checkmarks in the appropriate columns. Write a more positive alternative behavior in the right column. Add up your negative behavior totals each day so you can see your progress. Keep the completed forms and use them to see your progress over time.

Observe the Family Culture

OCD often takes advantage of the norms of a culture, taking them to the nth degree. A child's OCD bully can exploit a family's cultural norms. For example, in families where cleanliness is valued, contamination may be a big concern for the child with OCD. Families who value effort and achievement may have perfectionists on their hands. Religious families may have children who struggle with scrupulosity. Families who emphasize safety may have children who are overly careful and concerned about the possibility of accidents. We aren't saying this always happens or that the family values caused the OCD. We are saying that most children first develop their blueprints of what is important in life by observing their families, and the OCD bully nearly always targets those values and things that the individual holds dear.

Therefore, family values and norms, even reasonable ones, can provide a breeding ground for OCD concerns. Most cultural norms and rules are useful because the average person is somewhat careless, forgetful, and even lazy. Norms and values work against this natural tendency and so promote positive functioning in average people. But your child is not an average child; rather than inconsistently following the norms as non-OC children do, your child may consistently adhere to them, feeling extreme anxiety if the rules are violated.

For this reason, supporting your recovering child may necessitate modifying or abandoning certain accepted family beliefs, values, rules, or norms. First you must identify the values and rules that may be exploited by your child's OCD bully. Review the Family Culture Attitudes worksheet and check those values that you believe apply to your family and may be exploited by your child's OCD.

Family Culture Attitudes

☐ You should always wash your hands before eating.

☐ You should never eat off the floor or ground.

☐ You should brush your teeth after every meal.

☐ Cleanliness is next to godliness.

☐ You should always wear nice clothes.

☐ You should never wear clothes more than once without washing them.

☐ People judge you based on your appearance and performance.

☐ Your room should always be neat and clean.

☐ You should always do your best.

☐ You should get straight A's.

☐ Being the best is what's important.

☐ Your standards should be higher than those of others.

☐ Your work should always be neat.

☐ You should never do anything wrong.

☐ Haste makes waste.

☐ Never waste anything.

☐ You should never put anyone else at risk.

☐ You should never hurt anyone's feelings.

☐ A good person is a responsible person.

☐ You should never sit on a public toilet.

☐ You should always wash your hands after using the bathroom.

☐ You must eat and live in a healthy way.

☐ You should always look your best.

☐ Your hair should always be neat and clean.

☐ You should never wear dirty clothes.

☐ A cluttered desk indicates a cluttered mind.

☐ Your things should always be in order.

☐ You should try as hard as you can.

☐ You should not make mistakes.

☐ Grades indicate your level of success.

☐ Perfection is to be sought.

☐ Most mistakes are the result of carelessness.

☐ You should never wish people harm.

☐ Don't throw out things that can be recycled.

☐ Never throw out things you might need later.

☐ You should always do what's morally right.

☐ You should not harm anyone.

☐ You should not use the Lord's name in vain.

- [ ] God knows and judges your intentions as well as your actions.

- [ ] God is quick to judge.

- [ ] You should not swear or use bad language.

- [ ] You should never lie, cheat, or steal.

- [ ] Asking for or getting what you want is selfish.

- [ ] You should not be anxious.

- [ ] You should only think positive thoughts.

- [ ] You should always be strong.

- [ ] You should always follow your intuition or emotions.

- [ ] Thoughts are the same as actions.

- [ ] You should not get angry.

- [ ] Life should be easy.

- [ ] _____

- [ ] _____

- [ ] _____

- [ ] _____

- [ ] _____

- [ ] _____

- [ ] _____

- [ ] You should confess your mistakes and errors.

- [ ] God's rules must be followed exactly.

- [ ] You should always be kind and thoughtful.

- [ ] You should not be selfish.

- [ ] You should control your thoughts.

- [ ] People should not know you are anxious.

- [ ] Other people's opinions are very important.

- [ ] You should never let others see your weakness.

- [ ] Emotions indicate weakness.

- [ ] If you think it, it is the same as doing it.

- [ ] You should never let others down.

- [ ] No one should have to suffer.

- [ ] _____

- [ ] _____

- [ ] _____

- [ ] _____

- [ ] _____

- [ ] _____

- [ ] _____

Consider Other Family Problems That May Affect OCD

Your child is probably not the only person in your family with a problem. Unfortunately, almost any family issue can increase stress, which generally makes matters worse. Furthermore, if the other person's problem is OCD or another anxiety disorder that is not being treated, the potential impact is even greater. How can you possibly encourage one child to accept and cope with anxiety when someone else in the family is consistently avoiding it? As every parent knows, children seem to come equipped with hypocrisy meters. They will notice if they are being expected to work on their problem while others are not. A child in this situation will ask, "So and so has a problem, so why don't they have to do anything about it?"

To begin identifying important problems that other family members may have, look over the list below and check off any other problems that family members may have. The persons involved do not need to have a full-blown disorder to fuel resistance on the part of the child with OCD. To support the child's recovery, everyone must begin working on his or her problems.

Other Family Problems

☐ Marital conflict   ☐ Worrying

☐ Panic attacks   ☐ Social anxiety

☐ Agoraphobia   ☐ Trichotillomania

☐ Eating disorder   ☐ OCD

☐ Obsessive-Compulsive Personality   ☐ Depression
   Disorder (OCPD)

☐ Specific fear(s)   ☐ Smoking

☐ Drug use   ☐ Excessive alcohol use

☐ Poor anger control   ☐ Poor school performance

☐ Stealing or lying   ☐ Truancy

☐ Impoverished social activities   ☐ Low motivation to perform

☐ Lack of hobbies or interests   ☐ Irresponsibility

☐ Hostile attitude   ☐ Sibling conflict

Observe the Benefits of the OCD

It might surprise you to realize that OCD can sometimes have benefits for the person with OCD and for other family members. Frequently, the benefits of the OCD relate to the "other problems" you just checked off. Obsessive-compulsive disorder sucks up the entire attention of the family so that other problems just don't get their due attention. You may be skeptical, thinking, "What possible benefit could OCD give anyone?" Below are a few examples.

> An adult child has severe OCD that keeps him homebound. The parents have always intended to sell their home and move to Florida when their children leave home. While this is their dream, such a big change seems frightening and overwhelming to them. They are never forced to tackle this dream anyway—they can't sell the house because

the adult child can't possibly move out. (Benefits: the parents get to avoid facing their fear, and the child gets to continue living with his parents.)

An elementary-school age child has severe OCD. His OCD bully tells him he must stay home from school or he will become severely ill from germs. As a result he refuses to go to school and is homebound. In the family are two anxious adults who are also unable to leave the house. The child and these relatives spend many hours each day playing games. They think the child's problems are tragic but they enjoy the company. They joke together that they are all "neurotic." (Benefits: the relatives get to feel less alone, the child gets lots of attention, and they all get to avoid overcoming their problems.)

A teenagers's OCD takes up her father's entire life. He helps the child get off to school, stays on top of the school's staff to ensure she's being treated well and gets proper accommodations, and waits by the phone in case she calls in need of help. The father is at the OCD's beck and call. (Benefits: the father gets to avoid experiencing the anxiety and uncertainty that goes with taking risks and living a full life, and the child gets the complete attention of her father and is not expected to change.)

An adult who has had severe OCD for many years states, "If I got better, I'd need to get a life, start dating, go back to school—all the stuff I've wanted to do. It scares me to think about doing that." (Benefits: the person gets to avoid challenges that seem frightening.)

Recovery can sometimes require removing the benefits, both to the child and to the other family members. As long as benefits are in place, they'll probably decrease motivation to change. On the following Benefits of OCD chart, note whom you think benefits and how. Next, come up with solutions that might be tried (individually or as a family) to reduce these benefits. You will revisit these ideas in the next chapter when you develop a family plan.

Observe Family Ritual Participation and Avoidance Patterns

Tracking your child's rituals has probably illuminated how the OCD bully controls your family. The control operates in two ways: what family members *must do* and what they *must not do*. These are family "rituals" and family "avoidances." Eventually, removing family rituals and stopping family avoidances will be necessary for your child's recovery. Review your Observing OCD Behavior forms and, on a sheet of paper, make a list of avoidances and rituals family members participate in.

You'll want to bring a list of these demanded behaviors to your child's therapist because your child probably won't think of everything. You can expect that the therapist will work to integrate changes in these behaviors into your child's E/RP hierarchy. How

Benefits of OCD

Benefit and Beneficiary	Possible Solution to Eliminate Benefit
1.	1.
	2.
	3.
2.	1.
	2.
	3.
3.	1.
	2.
	3.

Chart 8d

soon they are targeted for work will be based on their difficulty, their importance to your child, and their importance to you.

To make sure your needs are considered, identify your priorities for the therapist. Remember, you'll be most helpful to your child when you are not burdened excessively by the demands your child makes. So make crawling out from under the most onerous tasks a priority sooner rather than later. Now, look at the items on the list you just made and prioritize them on the following Family Ritual and Avoidance Patterns worksheet. Plan to give this to your child's therapist.

Observe Your Child for Later Motivation Building

Part of your job as assistant coach is to motivate your child. It would seem that just getting relief from the OCD bully would provide enough motivation for your child to face the discomfort of treatment. It provides some motivation, but it's usually not enough. Therefore, you must identify what lights a fire under your child. You will use this information in the next chapter to arrive at productive agreements—contracts—with your child to reward him or her for taking on the "hard stuff."

To maximize your leverage, you need to know what your child values, which requires observing your child's life and choices including when he or she chooses to sleep. For a week or so, keep track of your child's routine, activities, and special requests on the Requests and Activities Observations chart. Track opposition on the Complaints and Arguments Observations chart. This information can provide valuable clues that can help you create tempting carrots to motivate your child.

This chapter has been aimed at helping you observe your child and family and notice how OCD affects everyone in the group. We hope that your attention has been sharpened and that you are now more aware of how your child's OCD bully affects family functioning and vice versa. You probably also have a better sense of what might motivate your child. How can you use this information to make a plan that will support your child's recovery? Answering this question will be the focus of chapter 9.

Family Ritual and Avoidance Patterns

List family rituals—behaviors the OCD requires of you or other family members—in order of their importance to you and other family members. At the top of the list should be the items that are most burdensome to you—the ones that you would like to eliminate earlier rather than later. (This order does not necessarily reflect the order in which the therapist will target these rituals. Removal of rituals will need to be integrated into your child's E/RP hierarchy.)

1.

2.

3.

4.

5.

6.

List family avoidances, those objects or activities that you or other family members avoid or abstain from because of your child's OCD. (These objects or activities may include things that directly trigger obsessions and also activities or situations that do not happen simply because they might be difficult for your child, such as a sibling having a sleepover, or the family traveling to Grandma's for a weekend.) Again, list in order of importance or oppressiveness to you and other family members.

1.

2.

3.

4.

5.

6.

Chart 8e

Requests and Activities Observations

Week of _____

	Special requests (for items, foods, activities, outings, or privileges)	Enjoyable activities (List activities and time spent.)	Rise time	Bed time	Curfew kept?
Sun.					
Mon.					
Tues.					
Wed.					
Thur.					
Fri.					
Sat.					

Chart 8f

Complaints and Arguments Observations

Week of _____

Complaints (about household rules and responsibilities)		Arguments observed (between child and other family members)			
		With whom?	About what?		
Sun.					
Mon.					
Tues.					
Wed.					
Thur.					
Fri.					
Sat.					

Chart 8g

Chapter 9

Developing a Family Plan, or Tying It All Together

Your work in chapter 8 revealed many areas where family functioning potentially has an impact on your child's OCD. For example, family culture may bolster the OCD bully's claims; silent benefits may reduce motivation to change; other family members' problems may flourish, providing an easy excuse for your child with OCD to resist change; or family rituals and family avoidances may directly strengthen your child's OCD. All of these observations suggest areas where changes in family functioning could support your child's efforts at recovery from OCD.

This chapter will help you create a way to make changes in your family's functioning that will support your child's recovery efforts. First, we will help you make family lifestyle changes that will give rewards and privileges more appeal to your child, and we'll help you arrive at rewards and privileges that will motivate your child. Second, we will help you to establish family meetings to provide a forum to discuss the changes that need to happen. Third, we will help you develop family contracts that will help you implement those changes in a gradual way.

We emphasize family work because, although you are not your child's therapist and are not equipped to direct your child's therapy, you can and should lead your family to create an environment that promotes growth for everyone. If everyone is expected to work toward personal goals on a weekly basis, then your child in therapy will not feel like the odd man out; hard personal work will be the family norm. The norm will create momentum in the family that will help to carry your child with OCD forward. Creating this plan will probably be difficult, but not as difficult as you might imagine. It will be easier if you don't expect perfection from anyone and you pace yourself and your family. Your main goal is to keep the family focused properly—taking steps, working methodically, and supporting change in everyone.

The process we advocate is simple. Hold a family meeting every week, and in that meeting establish a weekly contract for all family members. The family contract will specify goals (usually daily work) that each family member agrees to try to meet and also rewards for met goals. Each week, progress will be reviewed, successes will be rewarded, problems will be discussed, and new goals will be set. In time, the small steps your family takes should significantly reduce the problems you identified in chapter 8, and your child's recovery will be supported rather than hindered by the family.

Setting the Stage for a Reward System

Success of the plan to foster small consistent changes by each family member often hinges on the potency of the rewards offered. In this section we will consider rewards for children in general and some special issues for children with OCD. The first issue is the reason that rewards are so important. Many parents resist using rewards because they feel they are buying their children's cooperation.

Remember the adage, "You can catch more flies with honey than with vinegar." Don't be afraid to offer "honey," even to cooperative kids. In the plan we are advocating, you will be asking for change from every family member. You will need to offer rewards to your child working on OCD, and you will create sibling resentment if one child has the opportunity to earn goodies, while the other is left out. Change is hard and effortful, deserves reward, and probably will not happen without it. We wouldn't expect any adult to perform a difficult job day after day without receiving compensation. Let's not expect children to rise to a higher standard.

Rewards are especially important for children working on their OCD. The treatment of OCD requires great courage, hard work, and perseverance. In essence, it requires children to do exactly what every fiber of their being is telling them not to do. Plenty of children would rather deal with the devil they know (OCD) than take on one they don't (E/RP). Some may even claim that they really don't mind their OCD bully. Most of these children are suffering keenly, but fighting back is so frightening that they want no part of it.

For these children, intrinsic motivation is insufficient to get them to work. You get out of therapy what you put into it; so the more you do, the more you get back. For this reason, completing homework assignments is absolutely necessary if any change is to be accomplished. For reluctant children, parents need to make the work worthwhile by developing a reward schedule that will support their effort. Sonya hated her cluttered room, but she felt overwhelmed by fear of her anxiety, of giving up her collecting, and of deciding what to discard. She felt that she'd rather live with the OCD. External rewards gave her an added incentive to fight the OCD.

The first step is to think about generating a list of things that your children are itching to have right now. If you have children with chronic "wantitis," you are lucky because doing this will probably prove easy. However, some children have few wants, so identifying reinforcers for them is difficult. Often, this is an indication of a family system in which desires are immediately sated—the children don't want anything because they already have everything that they might want. Other times, this occurs because the children are not really "into getting stuff."

If your children's desires are routinely sated, the first step is to stem the flow of goodies. This may require limiting the gifts that your children receive from well-meaning relatives, no longer buying on impulse whenever you see something that your children might like, or saying no to impulsive requests that your children make. It may also mean deciding that activities your children have come to expect as their right (e.g., horseback riding lessons, tennis lessons, etc.) need to become earned activities. The unfortunate reality is that if your children are regularly getting whatever they desire, then there won't be any "stuff" they want and you will be hard put to find carrots to dangle. But when the goodie gates are lowered, usually "wantitis" reemerges and carrots become plentiful.

For children who care little about belongings, think about what interests them and try to come up with special experiences that are related to that interest—perhaps seeing a play, concert, or professional sports game. The kinds of rewards on wish lists and the earning structure you create will depend greatly on the child's age.

♦ **Level I: Young Children.** Young children (age six to eight) are the easiest to motivate using rewards. For these children, stickers and trinkets are usually sufficient to motivate daily work. The most effective strategy is to reward immediately following the work with a reinforcer (star or sticker and praise). At the end of the week, a certain number of stars or stickers can then be turned in for a big reward: a trinket or an inexpensive outing. Children with attention-related difficulties will require shorter intervals between rewards. You may need to experiment to find the timing that works best. However, young children with OCD and attention-related difficulties will probably need rewards for exposure work immediately upon completion and daily rewards for accomplished ritual prevention.

♦ **Level II: School-Age Children.** School-age children generally also respond well to keeping a chart that denotes daily completion of work with points (stars) and then working toward a larger reward with a designated point cost. Many parents come up with a price list for wanted items and experiences. The child earns a reward from this list when enough points are accumulated. Children this age tend to be less satisfied with trinkets and have more definite wants.

◇ **Level III: Tweens.** As children get older, they tend to have specific items that they want, but they are also savvy and will often try to take advantage of the system. Children of this age with OCD often try to negotiate to get the biggest reward for the least work and the least anxiety, forgetting the real reasons they want to get better. They need to be reminded often of their intrinsic reasons to change. Furthermore, most children in this age range tend to want big-ticket items (laptops, palm pilots, video game players, etc.). Often, when they have earned a prize, they lose interest in working and parents are left scrambling to find the next big item that will motivate them.

The solution is to have your child work toward having you buy *for yourself* the desired item. This way, your child is working just to get the desired thing into the house. Once you've bought the item for yourself, provide the child the opportunity to earn time on *your toy,* but use it periodically to further the impression that it belongs to you. Sonya's parents bought a video game player and kept it in the game room. An hour-long E/RP exercise that was rated as an 8 on her fear hierarchy earned her a half hour of use. An hour-long exercise that was rated a 4 on her fear hierarchy earned her fifteen minutes. The beauty of this system is that you can get continued mileage out of big-ticket items without having to endlessly buy new accessories or other items.

◇ **Level IV: Teens.** Teenagers generally don't respond as well to keeping charts and being rewarded with goodies. Frequently, they respond better to cold, hard cash. Teens can sometimes be motivated by receiving small cash rewards for completed goals and larger bonuses for maintaining gains in a noticeable way. Some parents like to reward when significant new gains become established behaviors (e.g., shortened showers or going to bed at a reasonable hour). A stepped reward system often works well. For example, you can pay various allowance amounts depending on the level of maintenance of E/RP goals or other goals. A teen with OCD who consistently gives in to urges to do a ritual and avoids exposure exercises might earn an allowance of *x* dollars a week for doing household chores, while that same child could earn twice that for completing the same chores when resisting rituals and practicing exposures.

Added privileges are often effective rewards for this age group. For example, teens could earn the right to stay out past their usual curfew or borrow the car. An added bonus to this system is that it prevents arguments because the expectations regarding certain privileges are clearly delineated.

Creative Rewards: Beyond Things

When children don't want "things" and are not interested in special outings, you will need to think harder to come up with motivators. There are two areas you can mine to discover possible reinforcers. One possible reward is to relax a hated household rule. For example, if your twelve-year-old child's bedtime is 9:00 P.M., the privilege of staying up until 9:30 or 10:00 could be earned. If an hour per day of computer playtime is permitted, an extra half hour could be earned. If television viewing is restricted, additional TV time could be earned. The second possibility is to redefine which activities in your family life are truly rights and which ones are privileges. Activities that the child considers to be part of normal life can be *redefined as privileges rather than rights,* and participation can then serve as a reward. For example, getting permission to participate in or attend a sports game could depend on whether the child satisfactorily adhered to the contract the day before.

Some parents are reluctant to use adherence to a contract as a precondition for participation in extracurricular activities. These parents may be too invested in their child being a sports star or performer, or they may feel their child's absence might "penalize" the other children on the team who are counting on the child. Parents often feel reluctant to deny a child with OCD his or her extracurricular activities, because these activities are sometimes the only situation where their child functions well. Quite reasonably, parents don't want to take away one of the few things in their child's life that seems to be working.

So if you won't be able to follow through with denying your child a treasured activity, then don't put it in the contract. Be honest with yourself about what you're comfortable withholding, and why. If your reluctance is due to your own personal investment in your child's success, you may need to rethink your priorities. Remember that OCD is a mean bully that can wreak havoc in your child's life; do you really want to allow this bully to thrive in order to preserve your vicarious glory? If you are concerned that keeping your child out of the activity would not be fair to your child's peers, consider whether fear of embarrassment and concern about the peers' anger might be enough to encourage him or her to follow through on the contract.

If your concern is that these activities are the only times when your child feels good and you don't want him or her to miss out, then we agree that it is painful to have to withhold a valued activity. Therefore, only withhold the activity if it's necessary. Use other reinforcers at your disposal first and see if they're potent enough. But if these other reinforcers don't do the trick, then you may have no choice. You may need to use participation in cherished activities as a motivator if there is really nothing else your child cares about.

The only time you should *not* make activities contingent on therapy work is when your child is very depressed and withdrawn socially (with OCD or not). In such cases, the activities should almost always be an ironclad part of the plan for healing because these pursuits may be the best antidote to their depression. For depressed and withdrawn children, participation in activities is usually a therapy goal.

As we've outlined above, the important preliminary tasks necessary to developing a reinforcement strategy are to observe your children and learn what they like and to implement structure and rules so that their desires are not automatically sated. In chapter 8, you collected information about your child's values and activities using the Requests and Activities worksheet and Complaints and Arguments worksheet, so that you would be prepared to identify potential reinforcers. Now, look at those worksheets and identify potential reinforcers; also look for any changes that need to be made to create a more structured household system that will promote leverage for you. Use the following Creating Carrots worksheet to help pull this information together.

Family Meetings

The backbone of family work will be the weekly family meeting. (The structure and intent of family meedtings proposed by this plan are adapted from the philosophy and structure of G.O.A.L.S. Support Group Meetings, Grayson 1997.) For the majority of families, these should take place regularly once a week for approximately an hour. It is very important that all family members be present—for this to be a family process, everyone must participate and work toward goals. The norm that you are establishing by holding these regular meetings is that the family places a value on active coping, problem solving, and growth work.

The purposes of the meetings are

◊ to identify each individual's personal goal for the week (complete new family contract)

◊ for the parents to clearly communicate one or two desired behaviors (target start behaviors) for each child to work at establishing, and to review consequences for unwanted behaviors when necessary (these issues will be discussed further in the next chapter)

◊ to review the family contract and goals attained from the previous week, and for parents to provide recognition and praise for accomplishments and provide tangible rewards as promised

◊ to problem solve obstacles to goal completion and to challenge thinking that might interfere with efforts

◊ to discuss any issues relevant to changes that are being worked toward

◊ to increase family cohesiveness and improve communication and relationships

The atmosphere of these meetings should be upbeat and supportive. The family meeting should not be a vehicle for humiliating, berating, or arguing. If rules or agreements have been violated during the week, then acknowledging the problem is useful, but *problem solving* should be the focus of the discussion. If the family meeting becomes a forum for disappointment, no one will want to come and the whole system will fall apart. To be effective, the parents must focus on shaping success. Assume that all are trying their best, look for evidence and actions that support this assumption, and give praise for small steps liberally. The "sandwich" technique works well—make suggestions for improvement only between positive comments that acknowledge effort or progress.

Creating Carrots

List the items that your child routinely requests. What are the prices of these items?

_____

_____

_____

If your child seems to want no items at all, list ways to make your environment a little less opulent. Consider stemming the flow of goodies into the house. If your child has too much, doesn't want anything, and doesn't take care of things, you can gradually reduce the abundance by establishing a rule that things that are not put away will be thrown away.

_____

_____

How much money are you prepared to spend per week to encourage work?

$ _____

Use your weekly monetary amount to determine the dollar value of the work you will require of your child to earn the items (e.g., if your amount is $20.00 per week, that would mean spending approximately $3.00 per day). Use this amount as a base to generate an exposure price list for the desired items, on a separate sheet of paper.

$ _____

List the house rules your child routinely complains about: _____

_____

_____

Would it be possible for you to relax any of these rules as a reward?

_____

_____

Chart 9a

Creating Carrots *(continued)*

Look at the arguments your child engages in with other siblings. Do conflicts routinely arise over the TV remote or use of the computer? Could you make control of these high-demand items for some period of time a reward that is earned by the child who has shown the most consistent work toward his or her weekly goal?

_____

_____

_____

List the activities that your child participates in. If your child is not depressed or socially withdrawn, would making this activity an earned privilege rather than a right provide motivation? In developing your reward schedule, you'll start with items, then move on to allowance, relaxation of rules, and then complaints. Only use the valued extracurricular activities when nothing else works.

_____

_____

_____

List below some changes you will make to increase your leverage now, prior to creating wish lists with your children during family meetings.

Schedule changes: _____

_____

_____

Entitlements that will become privileges: _____

_____

_____

Time limits on sedentary entertainments (TV, computer, video games):

_____

_____

Chart 9a—*continued*

Identifying Areas for Potential Work

The focus and structure of early family meetings will differ from family meetings that occur later on. These early meetings will focus on issues related to starting up. The first task is for family members to identify what they are going to work on. You will be prepared for these discussions because of the work you have already completed in chapter 8. As the parent, you can make suggestions and draw ideas from the Family Culture Attitudes, Other Family Problems, and Benefits of OCD worksheets. Establishing the process requires that each person be given the freedom and respect to decide for himself or herself what personal issues to tackle. As the process takes hold, family members will probably be able to provide input and feedback to other family members, especially if someone appears to be investing little effort and taking on unimportant goals. However, to begin with, each person's choice should be allowed to stand. Ideally, each person will choose a personally important problem. If you, as parent, believe that the goal is not important, you have the option to choose a reward commensurate with the anticipated investment of effort. However, remember that the initial goals chosen are less important than getting the process going. So don't get too bogged down in deciding where each person should start, and try to keep the process positive.

Making the Work a Priority: Scheduling

Once everyone has claimed an area to work on, then other important tasks must be accomplished. The first of these is to make the work a priority. Communicate clearly to children with OCD that you think weakening the OCD bully is their most important goal, which should take precedence over schoolwork and any other activity. The reason for this is simple: OCD has the potential to ruin everything else. If your child had cancer, you wouldn't think that maintaining grades or pursuing any other goal was more important than treatment. Stress the importance of your child's OCD work. For the other children, work toward goals identified in family meetings may not be their highest priority, but it still must be treated as important and one of their top responsibilities.

Part of communicating that change is a priority is encouraging all family members to schedule the work they need to accomplish. For your child with OCD, making progress requires a *minimum* of one hour a day of exposure practice (more is better!) in addition to ongoing ritual prevention work. For a younger child, you will need to schedule time in his or her day for practice. Family members without OCD must also schedule time to meet the goals that they have made for the week. In short, scheduling makes the work a priority. If in the process of scheduling this work, individuals discover that they are too busy, then they need to begin eliminating activities to make time. Without scheduling, the work of change will inevitably take a backseat to other scheduled activities in the day.

Identifying Reasons to Change

Next, focus on building motivation to change in all family members. Early meetings can be used to help family members identify the benefits of working on the identified problems (OCD and other difficulties). During one of your first family meetings, have all family members complete the Reasons to Change worksheet, which follows. We encourage everyone to identify ways in which life will be better when these problems are addressed. Post these lists where your family can regularly see them. Everyone needs to know what is wanted in the near future so that encouragement and reminders of the benefits of change can be offered when anyone is struggling.

Develop a Timeline for Removing Family Rituals and Avoidances

Early on in the family meetings, you will want to develop a timeline for the removal of OCD-related family rituals and avoidances. The family goal is to eventually stop all ritualistic and avoidant behavior. Continuing these behaviors strengthens the OCD bully and protects your child from carrying the full burden of the disorder, which diminishes the motivation to change. Ideally, your child will control the pace of when these changes occur by choosing the needed steps as therapy homework and as his or her weekly family goal as he or she goes along. However, sometimes children (and adults!) drag their heels in treatment, concentrating on the "easy" tasks over the harder ones, which tend to be more beneficial.

In these cases a timeline for removing family rituals and avoidances can help to keep the process moving. We have provided the Establish a Timeline for Removal of Rituals to assist you with this. This timeline consists of dates (deadlines) by which the family will begin to do things differently whether the child feels ready or not. A choice is created for the child: either prepare for and be strong enough to deal with the change when it occurs, or procrastinate and feel unready and anxious when the deadline arrives. The net effect of these deadlines is that they keep the therapy moving for reluctant recoverers. For the majority of children, deadlines come and go uneventfully because behavior change has already occurred.

The timeline should follow the pace of the child's therapy. In chapter 8, we encouraged you to identify and rank in order of importance to you and other family members the rituals and avoidances that your child's OCD bully foists upon your family. Hopefully, you've provided this information to your child's therapist. At some point, ask the therapist for a recommendation of the order in which these family rituals and avoidance patterns should be addressed and an estimated date for removing the behavior. Because you don't want to push too hard, a good rule of thumb is to pick dates a few weeks after the therapist's predicted times.

If you have no therapist, you will have to work with your child to rank the order in which to remove rituals and avoidances. Ask your child how anxiety provoking or difficult he or she expect the change to be. Ask for an estimate of what his or her fear temperature

Reasons to Change

Family member: _____

Problem: _____

What do I hate about this problem?	**How will life be better when this problem is addressed?**
1.	1.
2.	2.
3.	3.
4.	4.
5.	5.
6.	6.
7.	7.
8.	8.
9.	9.
10.	10.

Chart 9b

(1 to 10, with 10 being "out of control") would be if the change were to happen today, so that you are sure that you understand. Then, using the rank ordering, come to an agreement regarding when he or she will be willing to let go of each family behavior. If the child refuses to pick a date, make it clear you will choose for him or her. Do not be surprised if the child's chosen dates are far in the future. That's okay, within reason. Don't push for change too soon or too fast. On the other hand, be clear that waiting for years is not an option.

Let these deadlines, once committed to, become pretty much written in stone so that your child believes in them. The therapist is the only one who should have the power to change these deadlines once they're established. You must periodically remind your child of upcoming deadlines so that he or she has some idea of when you will be changing your behavior. Neglecting to inform or remind your child of these deadlines will guarantee the loss of the motivating function of the deadlines.

Creating Wish Lists or Reward Strategies

The final issue that needs to be addressed to get the process going is to work out a reward system for each family member (particularly the children). Ideally, you've had the chance to stem the flow of goodies into your home and create a more structured environment so that you have more bargaining power. During a family meeting, have everyone write down what they are wanting. If they have no ideas, refer to your Requests and Activities worksheet and Complaints and Arguments worksheet from chapter 8 to remind them of things they have asked for or wanted. Know ahead of time what you are prepared to spend and what you are prepared to do (see the Creating Carrots worksheet earlier in this chapter). Use this information to arrive at an agreement with each child using the ideas that we discussed earlier in this chapter.

The Family Contract

Once all of the initial business is taken care of, family meetings will begin to focus on the work of change. The vehicle for change is the family contract. Every week, each family member will commit to working on a goal that furthers the desired change process and will be promised a reward for accomplishing that goal. Over time, slowly but surely, change has to happen, provided that the family contracts are implemented effectively.

Family contracts are most effective when parents do not nag or police. It is best to let the rewards, or lack of rewards, do most of the talking. Your job as parent is simply to abide by the contract and liberally praise any success you observe during and outside of family meetings. Family contracts will only be as powerful as your word is good. Sometimes parents are tempted to yank an earned reward because of some other unrelated bad behavior on the part of the child. Yanking a reward (especially when done regularly) can sabotage the system because it destroys the belief that the carrot is attainable. Instead, be

Establish a Timeline for Removal of Rituals

List rituals and avoidances from easiest to remove to hardest. For items that are tied, determine the order based on how important the item is for you or other family members. Obtain from your child's therapist an estimated date on which to remove the ritual or begin confronting the avoidance. To establish removal time, add one to two weeks to the therapist's estimated date to allow extra time if needed. When you have your dates, write them on the family calendar so the dates are not forgotten.

Ritual or avoidance	Fear temperature (1 to 10, 10=worst)	Estimated date of readiness	Removal date
_____	_____	_____	_____
_____	_____	_____	_____
_____	_____	_____	_____
_____	_____	_____	_____
_____	_____	_____	_____
_____	_____	_____	_____
_____	_____	_____	_____
_____	_____	_____	_____
_____	_____	_____	_____
_____	_____	_____	_____
_____	_____	_____	_____
_____	_____	_____	_____
_____	_____	_____	_____
_____	_____	_____	_____
_____	_____	_____	_____
_____	_____	_____	_____

Chart 9c

very clear up front about rules or expectations that must be followed for the reward to actually be given. Be explicit about any "givens" that are important to you.

However, contract effectiveness will be diminished if you have too many rules or expectations tied to the reward. Folding too many rules into the contract will make it too hard for family members to succeed. At first, Sonya's parents added so many rules to the family contract that she never seemed to earn time playing video games. When they recognized that fighting OCD needed to be the top priority, they removed all other expectations so that completion of E/RP exercises guaranteed her time on the video game player.

Finally, there is a principle that is important for you to understand: *Reward or punishment aimed at "just stopping" OC behavior will probably fail.* It's wrong to assume that your child could stop OC behavior without too much trouble if only he or she wanted to. As was said earlier, OC behaviors are driven by anxiety and fear and do not occur because your child *wants* to do them. Therefore, indiscriminately rewarding non-OC behavior, or punishing avoidances or rituals, is not likely to work because the fear will still be more important to the child than any rewards or punishments you could offer. However, rewards and consequences can be useful tools *when they are tied to the therapy work.* Remember that therapy proceeds along a hierarchy; each homework assignment is undertaken when the child agrees that a task is doable—not necessarily easy, but doable.

Once the family-meeting system is established, meetings will tend to be similar, consisting primarily of establishing new goals for the week (the family contract) and solving problems related to goals that were not met. Since success relies on meeting small weekly goals, you need some understanding of how to set workable goals. For the most part, attainable goals will be (1) small (representing a small change that feels doable); (2) active (consisting of doing something rather than not doing something; in the case of ritual prevention, this means actively inviting uncertainty rather than doing a ritual); and (3) clear (specific and well-defined rather than vague, e.g., "I will take a walk every day" versus "I will feel better").

Setting Goals for the Child with OCD

The weekly goal for your child with OCD will usually be his or her weekly homework assignment from therapy. These goals may be specific E/RP tasks or they may be goals to permit the family to stop a family ritual or avoidance. Sometimes, the goal will be set because the child and therapist have selected that step. Other times, the family will need to set the goal because a deadline from the timeline for removing family rituals and avoidances has arrived. Remember, deadline effectiveness depends heavily on the family following through on these dates and working the goals into the family contract when the special days arrive. So stay in touch with your calendar and keep your child apprised of when changes will happen.

Setting Goals for Other Family Members

Setting goals for other family members is more difficult because the responsibility of generating ideas will largely fall to you. Let's review some of your findings from chapter 8 and discuss what needs to happen in the following areas.

Other family members' problems. First, there is the issue of other family members' problems. Some of these problems may be clinical problems that also require therapy. If that person is not in therapy, weekly goals can consist of taking steps to start. If the person is already in therapy, use the therapy homework for weekly goals so that the process mirrors the process of the child with OCD. If the "other problem" is more of a life issue that does not require therapy, or if you do not have access to a therapist, try to think small and discuss with that family member what would represent a step forward that is doable. Always aim for one small step at a time. If you are the person with the problem, do the same thing for yourself. If you find it too difficult to identify where to start, consider finding professional help.

Benefits of OCD. Another area discussed in chapter 8 has to do with the benefits of OCD, often a good area to work on. Discuss with the family member involved the apparent benefits and the possible solutions that you've already considered. Together you will need to arrive at ways to break these solutions into small steps or come up with alternative solutions that he or she likes better. Remember, benefits can rarely be eliminated in one week, and sometimes professional help is needed. Oftentimes, perseverance is the most important ingredient to finding solutions; keep looking until you find a solution that works.

Family attitudes. One of the issues we assessed in chapter 8 is whether or not particular family attitudes were supporting the obsessive concerns of your child with OCD. Tackling these attitudes can yield weeks of goals for many family members. After you identify the relevant attitudes, as you did on the Family Culture Attitudes form, the challenge becomes changing them. This relates to the concept of "letting go of normal," discussed previously. In essence, look for ways to "break the rules." In the movie, *The Royal Tenenbaums,* the title character, Royal, teaches his grandchildren to run across the street when the sign says "Do Not Cross," to shoplift, and to hitch a ride on a garbage truck. Of course, we do not advocate taking the idea that far, but you might suggest breaking the cleanliness rule by encouraging people to shower less frequently or practice eating with dirty hands. But don't encourage changes before your child with OCD is ready for them.

Use goals to model new behaviors. Keep in mind, to reduce the effect of family culture, you personally need to go beyond lip service to implement these changes and work toward the relevant goals yourself, acting as a role model. When other family members follow suit, the whole family will essentially be engaging in E/RP exercises. Rodney's family was very safety conscious, so avoiding chemicals and harsh cleaning agents seemed like just another commonsense precaution. To support Rodney's treatment, the whole family took on the goal to use these chemicals daily and to leave them out in plain view.

Many non-OCD-affected people balk at the idea of engaging in E/RP exercises. They think that since they don't have the problem they should not be doing the extreme stuff. You too might be thinking, "My rules work for me." We are not disputing that your rules work for you or even that your rules are correct. We suggest this strategy so that you might create and maintain a supportive environment that will help create momentum for your child. Every year, Dr. Jon Grayson and Dr. Fitzgibbons run a camping trip for groups of people with OCD. They also host an annual "Virtual Camping" workshop at the National OCF Conference. The rule for both the camping trip and the workshop is that everyone participates in all E/RP exercises regardless of whether the exercise has anything to do with their individual OCD symptoms. Having everyone participate in every exercise is powerfully supportive to the individuals attempting to confront what they fear.

Modeling creates momentum for the person who is actually facing a fear. When people see other people doing something, they are more likely to believe they can attempt it. If the people doing the modeling are experiencing some anxiety, then the modeling is that much more powerful because it is an example of someone actually mastering a fear. For this reason, the fact of family members breaking a family norm and experiencing some anxiety (even when it is not comparable to the anxiety experienced by the person with OCD) is likely to be powerfully supportive. Hopefully, breaking a family norm *will* create some discomfort in non-affected family members—anxious models make the best models.

Family members should avoid minimizing the changes with claims of safety, saying, "See, this is safe. We can do it." The idea behind changing the rules should be to weaken the need for certainty. Saying it's safe diminishes the message, which should be "We as a family are willing to take this risk, not because we're sure it's safe, but because we believe the benefit of weakening the OCD bully is more important than the risk we're taking."

Other Goals for the Child with OCD and Other Family Members

Consider the impact of OCD on relationships within the family, and set goals aimed at repairing damage done by OCD. The havoc of OCD can often erode relationships within a family because of conflict or frustration. You will find that as your child improves the conflict abates, although residual hard feelings and distance can remain in relationships that were once close. Oftentimes, the best antidote to this problem is for the individuals involved to set a goal to participate in some regular activity together for a number of weeks so that they have the opportunity to reconnect.

When your family is ready, make copies of the blank Family Contract form and fill one out at each weekly family meeting.

Problem Solving around Unattained Goals

Toward the beginning of our discussion of family meetings we pointed out that one important activity in each family meeting is examining and solving problems related to goals that are not met. The truth of the matter is that many times goals will not be met, because old patterns are hard to break and few people like to change.

Paying attention to this issue communicates to all family members the value and importance given to efforts to change. If someone repeatedly does not fulfill his or her part of the contract and no attention is given to this fact, then it's likely that the whole

Family Contract

Week of _____

Family member: _____

Goals: _____

_____

_____

Rewards: _____

_____

_____

Family member: _____

Goals: _____

_____

_____

Rewards: _____

_____

_____

Family member: _____

Goals: _____

_____

_____

Rewards: _____

_____

_____

Chart 9d

family will begin to think that family meetings and contracts are a charade. How you handle this problem will make or break your family meetings.

Do maintain the assumption that everyone wants to change and cares about his or her goals. Don't jump to the conclusion that a person just doesn't want to change. If you can maintain a positive attitude, then you'll be supporting the healthy part of the person and will be more likely to identify problems and come up with solutions. In essence, the message you want to communicate is, "Getting stuck is a normal problem. Let's try to find a way to solve it."

The first step in addressing this issue is to ask, nonjudgmentally, "What got in the way?" "What was hard about this?" You want to identify the reasons for either trying and failing or not trying at all. Sometimes the problem will be that the step was too big or too hard and the person underestimated the difficulty. In that case, a smaller step should be identified. At other times logistical, but solvable, problems will have gotten in the way. You may find that the incentive was not great enough, in which case you may need to increase the reward.

You will often discover that the reasons for not fulfilling a goal are really thinking problems: predictions of outcomes (catastrophizing, fortune-telling) that get in the way of trying; assessments of performance (overgeneralization, all-or-nothing thinking) that are demoralizing; fear of what others might think (mind reading); feeling like a dope, jerk, or loser (labeling); or feeling too scared to try (emotional reasoning). These thinking barriers are the same kinds of unhelpful thinking patterns that we reviewed in chapter 7.

Approach these barriers by helping the family member identify the obstacle or excuse, encouraging everyone to identify the kind of unhelpful thought it represents, and then using the challenging questions in chapter 7 to find an objective response that works better. Emphasize helping everyone to shift their thinking so that it supports efforts at changing.

To help you in this process, we've provided the Working through Obstacles worksheet that follows. Keep in mind that this exercise should not be used to challenge the OC thinking itself. The exercise is most useful when it supports the effort of making changes, not when it is used to convince a person that an action is actually safe.

Working through Obstacles

Date: _____

Goal for week: _____

Obstacles (What got in the way? What was hard about the goal?): _____

_____

_____

_____

Thoughts that got in the way (What kind of thinking problem was it?): _____

_____

_____

_____

Answers to challenging questions from chapter 7: _____

_____

_____

_____

_____

More realistic thoughts to practice: _____

_____

_____

_____

Solutions or new plan to try for next week: _____

_____

_____

_____

Chart 9e

In this chapter we have focused on helping you create a system for implementing changes and fostering family momentum to support your child's recovery. In time, many of the problems you identified in chapter 8 will resolve because of your family's methodical and consistent goal-by-goal work. We don't promise that this process will be easy—in fact, it will probably be quite challenging, because change is hard for everyone. But these changes are doable and the process we advocate can help your family prove it. Remember, be gentle with everyone, stay positive, and stay focused. The process will go more smoothly when you take mistakes and stumbles in stride and keep your sense of humor. Remember, an important aspect of the support you are offering your child is the understanding that everyone has problems that need work, that he or she is not alone.

In the next chapter, we'll turn our attention to helping you reestablish parental skills that may have fallen by the wayside since the OCD took up residence in your house. It's likely that in the chapters that follow you'll continue to gather ideas for goals for all family members that can be incorporated into your family's new growth process.

Chapter 10

Parenting through the Process

Parents of children with OCD are often tempted to stop their normal parenting practices, believing that their children require something different. We disagree. All children need their parents to be, first and foremost, their parents. And children with OCD may frequently require *more* parenting than children without. The parenting strategies that work for non-OC children also work for OC children, but you may need to proceed more slowly, hang in there longer, and repeat the strategies more to see the same effects. In this chapter we'll help you adjust normal parenting practices to fit your child with OCD.

What All Children Need

All children need a loving relationship with their parents. They need parents who make decisions that are in the child's best interests, spend time with them regularly, treat them with respect and kindness, and communicate to them regularly that they are valued and loved unconditionally. This communication of love and value should be explicit: regularly saying, "I love you," "You are important to me," and "You are a terrific kid." Just as important are the actions that communicate your message louder than words: spending time with your child on a daily basis even when you have other tasks weighing on your mind, encouraging your child when he or she is discouraged, listening to whatever he or she has to say, and kissing your child good night even when you are thoroughly disgusted at his or her behavior.

Dr. Aureen Pinto Wagner (2002), in her book *What to Do When Your Child Has Obsessive-Compulsive Disorder: Strategies and Solutions,* recommends spending "YAMA time" (you and me alone time) on a daily basis to promote loving relationships between parents and children. What she suggests is a minimum of fifteen minutes per day devoted to "just hanging" (preferably not in front of the TV!) with your child. We wholeheartedly endorse this recommendation as a beginning step in developing the solid parental relationship children require.

All children need the security that comes with having reasonable limits on their behavior. They need to know the parent is in charge and making the decisions. Children feel secure when they can trust that the parent is in control and will calmly enforce the family's limits and rules. Rules and limits need to be reasonable and fair and need to be in the child's best interest. Security comes from knowing that the limits are stable and constant. The more control over their own limits children exercise, particularly when their emotions are determining that control, the less secure they feel. There are three reasons for this:

1. Deciding their own limits is too much responsibility for children, so it can feel overwhelming to them.

2. If children are in charge, they must look to themselves to provide safety and security, and that means that safety and security can no longer be assumed.

3. Children who set their own limits tend to exert their control based on whatever emotions they are currently feeling; every child knows how precarious their own emotions feel, so while this power may seem rewarding to them for the moment, in the long run their lives feel out of control.

Children need parents who consistently behave as adults. Children are reactive because they do not have the maturity to calmly handle their own or other people's strong emotions. In contrast, parenting often requires unflappable rationality. There is no room for emotions taking over; that's when things are said and done that parents regret later. When parents react with anger during a heated moment, they tend to threaten with severe punishment. When they calm down they may relent and not follow through on their extreme threats. Thus, reactive parenting leads inevitably to inconsistency. The cost is that parents eventually lose credibility with their children and compliance with rules and limits declines. Sadly, such a pattern costs parents their child's respect, which erodes the parent-child relationship and does not provide a useful model of emotional maturity for the child to aspire to.

Children require structure, particularly in the form of regular schedules. Early on, many parents begin to rely on their children's behavior or stated preferences in deciding mealtimes and bedtimes, resulting in often irregular eating and sleeping patterns. Dr. Fitzgibbons has seen many children who, at the age of five, are eating on demand at erratic times and going to bed as late as midnight. The parents lament that the children won't eat or sleep at set times. They also frequently complain that their children are difficult to manage.

These children's unmanageability is the result of several factors. Many children become more active when they are tired, so if a parent uses this cue to determine whether or not children are tired enough to sleep they are likely to be misled. Children, particularly young ones, often do not recognize when they are hungry or when they are tired until the feelings are extreme. They can have meltdowns simply because they are hungry and do not realize it. Tired children are less able to deal with the frustrations of daily life, let alone the challenges of OCD. They are frequently irritable and have a decreased ability to concentrate. The solution to these problems is often simply to establish a schedule or routine for your child.

The ability to recognize internal cues for hunger and fatigue improves with maturity and with more regular circadian rhythms, the body's natural tendency to be awake at certain times and to be sleepy at others, hungry at certain times and not at others. Eating and sleeping patterns are strongly related and both influence the child's natural circadian rhythms. Erratic schedules create erratic circadian rhythms. We are all wired to establish these rhythms; however, some people tend to have more erratic patterns than others. When a child is on a regular eating and sleeping schedule, his or her system—even for a child with a naturally erratic pattern—is more likely to establish regular rhythms. A child who is not on a relatively routine schedule does not get to train his or her body to follow a regular pattern, and the child's behavior and happiness usually suffer.

Many sleep and behavior problems can be reduced and sometimes even eliminated simply by establishing a routine schedule for eating and sleeping. Sleep requirements do vary among individuals. However, on average they range from eleven hours per night for a six-year-old to eight hours and fifteen minutes per night for an eighteen-year-old. If your child is consistently getting less than these amounts of sleep per night, then you probably need to establish a routine so your child can get more sleep. For more help, read *Solve Your Child's Sleep Problems* by Richard Ferber (2004).

Refining Parenting Practices

Most children with OCD are and want to be "good kids." Many, however, struggle with anger and irritability. Some have developed a habit of throwing tantrums. Anger and irritability are frequently side effects of living with OCD. Think about it: how do you feel when you are in a room with a radio pounding, people demanding something from you, and a television blaring? Thinking, listening, and functioning are extremely difficult because of all the extraneous noise. In such circumstances you probably feel angry and stressed and want to scream, "Be quiet!" because you can't hear yourself think. This is similar to how children with OCD frequently feel. It's hard for them to think, focus, and concentrate because there is so much noise going on in their head. So much of their resources are devoted to filtering out the noise that they just don't have the patience that a non-affected child might demonstrate.

There's a second contributor to the anger your child may display. Many children with OCD have lived with extreme anxiety for a long time and may have discovered that when they are distressed their parents will shift their limits. When this is the case, the result can be that the child's distress rules the household. Sometimes, the distress takes on a life of its own. The household revolves around keeping the child calm and expectations are abandoned in order to pacify the child. Under these circumstances, tantrums and demands can become a way of life.

Discipline

The first discipline principle has to do with establishing your leadership. Your goal until your child reaches approximately age twelve is to clearly establish that you are in charge. This means that your family cannot run as a democracy. The parents must lead; they need to set the limits and enforce the consequences. Parents can listen to their children and consider their preferences, but decisions need to be based on the parents' judgments of what is best for their children with regard to safety, growth, and development. Parental expectations must be tailored to the resources, abilities, and difficulties of each particular child. Once expectations are established, parents can't afford to modify them just because their child has launched a successful and persuasive campaign. Limits can't be negotiable, or you will have a child who perpetually challenges your decisions.

The second principle is that parenting is all about flexibility, not rigidity. The right limit for one child may or may not be the same as that for another child. Children differ and the limits they require differ as well. The goal for all parents is to shape their child into a rational, self-regulating, responsible person who has the emotional tools to build a contented, productive life and to deal with life's inevitable problems.

This process will happen gradually over the course of many years and requires building in small steps. Setting rigid limits because something is right will not be effective if you have not taken into account the idiosyncrasies, capabilities, and challenges of your particular child. You will succeed by establishing expectations and limits that take into account both where you want your child to wind up and where he or she is currently. The process involves shaping, reinforcing any small change in the desired direction, and waiting for mastery of one step before the next is tackled. Shaping requires first and foremost that you pay attention to and praise the desired behaviors you see in your child rather than simply focusing on his or her misbehavior or on desired behaviors you are not seeing.

The third principle is one of the paradoxes of parenting: you must work to establish control so that you can effectively let go of all control. Parenting is all about letting go; first they are in the womb, then they are not; they nurse constantly, then they stop; they are with you all the time, then you send them off to school. You are their world; then their friends are their world; finally you say good-bye.

If you have not established that you are in charge by the time your children are ten to twelve years old, if they have not internalized the values you have taught, you have a much harder hill to climb. Your next task, which begins when your children are around age eleven and continues well after they leave home, is to gradually let go and let them assume control of their lives. Parents must slowly relinquish their control and decision-making authority to their children. When the child handles increased freedom responsibly, that becomes the signal to the parent to give a little more freedom. A child's not handling freedom responsibly is the signal to either back up or wait until the proper use is mastered.

Discipline Strategies

Every parent needs strategies for discipline. Without them, the parent has no system to rely on and will inevitably revert to reactive parenting. A full discussion of discipline is beyond the scope of this book. However, we will review some guidelines here. Problems that parents experience usually have to do with two related kinds of behaviors. One kind comprises the behaviors that you would like your child to do, or "start" behaviors: doing therapy homework and school homework, putting things away, practicing an instrument, and so on. The other comprises the behaviors you would like your child not to do, or "stop" behaviors: yelling, screaming, hitting, demanding stuff, instigating arguments, and so on. Start and stop behaviors are often closely related in that for every behavior you want your child to stop, there is an accompanying desired start behavior that could be substituted.

Reinforcements to encourage start behaviors. Generally, to establish start behaviors parents should use reinforcements, or rewards, such as earned privileges, money allowances, special activities, and liberal attention and praise. A common mistake that many parents make is to overlook and take for granted all the positive things their children do. Noticing this good behavior and appreciating it is the first step toward encouraging more of the behaviors that you want to see. When a child becomes hooked on positive attention, he or she will want to please you more and will be more inclined to tackle other start behaviors. When first attempting to establish a start behavior, you may need to rely on extrinsic reinforcements (goodies); as the behavior becomes established you will rely more on verbal reinforcements and shift the extrinsic reinforcements to other, more difficult start behaviors.

Time-outs to discourage stop behaviors. The most effective tools for stop behaviors are natural consequences, logical consequences, and time-out procedures. Many parents who come to therapy report that their children do not respond to time-outs. A few words about this may be helpful. First, time-outs are most useful when disciplining children twelve and under. As a child matures (starting around age ten or eleven), parents need to begin using natural and logical consequences more often. Second, time-outs should not be considered punishments but rather should be viewed as an opportunity for the child to get control of his or her behavior. A good rule of thumb for the length of time for a time-out is generally one minute for every year of your child's age. Begin timing after the child is in the time-out location and not engaging with the parent.

Generally, when time-outs are not effective it is because they have been implemented poorly. They are most effective when parents are consistent, firm, and not reactive. They are almost always ineffective when the child has engaged the parent in argument or negotiation or when the time-out is given after the parent has already become angry. Time-outs must be implemented before the child has successfully pressed the parent's buttons. To learn more about how to effectively implement time-out procedures, we highly recommend the book *1-2-3 Magic: Effective Discipline for Children 2–12,* by Thomas W. Phelan, Ph.D. (1996). It provides numerous useful scenarios showing how children may counter the time-out procedure. It also helps parents to understand these situations and respond more effectively so that the strategy will work.

Natural consequences to discourage stop behaviors. When you use natural consequences as a discipline strategy, you are letting the world teach your child for you. As your child grows, it is often preferable to sidestep a power struggle and simply let your child experience the natural consequence that follows from a poor decision. This approach affords the child the opportunity to learn that every action has a consequence, allows him or her to learn personal responsibility, and eliminates the risk of your losing a power struggle. Repeatedly losing power struggles with your child erodes your base of authority, so this outcome is to be avoided as much as possible.

Additionally, the more children experience natural consequences, the more likely it is that they will actually begin considering the possible results of their actions before they act. Rather than argue with a twelve-year-old about wearing proper clothing, let her be cold. Sidestep the nightly power struggle with a thirteen-year-old over doing his homework, and let him experience some failure. Don't nag to get a sixteen-year-old out of bed in the morning; instead let her miss the bus and get to school under her own steam.

Logical consequences to discourage stop behaviors. Relying on natural consequences is not always possible or advisable because the circumstances may be impractical, dangerous, or insufficiently aversive. An example of an insufficiently aversive consequence might be when a child does not do his homework and receives a low grade but does not seem to care. An example of a dangerous natural consequence would be the car accident that could result from permitting your child to drive while under the influence of alcohol. An example of an impractical natural consequence would be letting your child miss the bus when there is no accessible pedestrian route to school.

In such circumstances, parents need to rely on logical consequences, which are consequences that are logically related to the problem at hand. For example, a report card littered with D's and F's because a child hasn't been doing homework might suggest too many extracurricular activities. A logical consequence could be to drop out of basketball until the end of the season so that more time can be devoted to homework. A child who drinks and drives could be required to entertain friends at your home so that you can supervise their social activities. A child who misses the bus and needs you to drive him or her because it is too far to walk could be charged a fee for your service.

As we mentioned earlier, sometimes parents of children with OCD become so consumed by their child's symptoms that they stop leading their family. Rather than the parent being in charge, distress is calling all of the shots. In such cases, discipline seems to be a hopeless endeavor. These parents often believe discipline does not work with their child. But children with OCD are still children, with the same needs and tendencies as other children. They respond to the same parental strategies. As we said earlier, sometimes they require *more* parenting. If you ahve not been using a discipline strategy, then establishing one will be challenging but imperative. Understand that your child will not respond at first. The behavior will inevitably get worse before it improves. Your child will likely push you to see if you will be as good as your word. However, if you calmly persist and don't back down, children with OCD will respond just like other children. Count on it.

Setting Expectations and Limits

By far the hardest part of parenting a child with OCD is deciding what limits and expectations to set. the difficulty boils down to two issues: deciding what to focus on and when; and discriminating what is OCD and should be accommodated and what is simply unwanted behavior.

As always, the first step is to try to assess where your child is now relative to where you would like your child to be. To do this, you will need to think about what you would expect of your child and what limits you would set *if your child did not have* OCD. Doing so requires comparing your child with OCD to children who do not have this problem. We are not saying that you should currently expect the same things of your child as you would of a child without OCD. Instead, you need to get an idea of how much work needs to be done for your child to become more functional. Remember, one of your long-term goals is for your child to become a functional adult. The best way to help him or her get there is to shape your child's behavior so that he or she becomes a functional child who is able to handle expectations and limits that are age appropriate.

To begin the process of deciding what to focus on first, use the Brainstorming Possible Expectations and Limits worksheet that follows to identify possibilities. You may find it helpful to also complete one of these sheets for each of your other children. If you are not sure what expectations are age appropriate, feel free to consult your child's therapist and use the resources that are available to you—think about your other non-affected children, your children's friends, and your friends' children, and identify expectations they routinely meet.

Next, consider each possibility more fully. For each expectation, write down the desired start behavior and the accompanying stop behavior. Ask your child to determine how difficult or stressful he or she finds the desired behavior (1=easy or not stressful; 10=very difficult or most stressful). Indicate whether he or she currently does the start behavior with a "yes" (sometimes to frequently) or "no" (never). This is important information because it indicates whether the child has mastered the behavior and it is part of his of her repertoire. Indicate whether the performance of the desired behavior is erratic because of entanglement with OCD ("yes"=more difficult and performed less because of

OCD; "no"=performance is unrelated to OCD; "sometimes"=performance is sometimes negatively affected by OCD). Decide whether or not you can deal with or consistently tolerate the existing stop behavior ("yes"=can tolerate; "no"=not acceptable ever). Anything that you can't tolerate without having a strong emotional reaction should be definitely identified as an unacceptable behavior that comes with a consequence. Finally, prioritize these expectations according to the order of importance for your child's well-being. Consider the order of the items in the list below when establishing these priorities.

1. Limits and expectations associated with health and safety issues such as diabetes management, curfews, drinking and driving, substance abuse, riding bicycles without a helmet, violence, nutrition, and self-destructive behaviors such as cutting, purging, etc.

2. Expectation to follow through on therapy work

3. Expectation to maintain a reasonable schedule: regular meal times, bedtimes, and rise times

4. Expectation to attend school

5. Limits associated with major behavioral control problems, breaking things for example.

6. Expectations related to schoolwork

7. Expectations related to household chores

8. Limits associated with minor behavioral control problems, yelling, arguing, and other disrespectful behavior, for example

9. Expectations related to age-appropriate personal responsibility

10. Expectations related to work associated with religious activities and music, dance, and sports lessons

Review your list of target start and stop behaviors. Many of the priorities listed above may not even appear on your list. If this is the case, it probably indicates that you are already seeing desired behaviors in your child. Praise your child regularly for the fact that he or she actually does a lot of what you want or expect already.

From the start behaviors you have listed, select one or two desired target start behaviors that you, the parent, will identify during the family meeting as an expectation you have for your child in the upcoming weeks. Your expectation is that your child will work on this target start behavior in addition to whatever personal goal he or she has chosen. To select which start behavior on your Brainstorming worksheet should be the one that you will request from your child, weigh the rank of importance of the desired behaviors against the information that you've indicated in the other columns of the Brainstorming worksheet.

Brainstorming Possible Expectations and Limits

Start/ Desired behavior	Stop/ Undesirable behavior	Rank of importance of start behavior for the good of the child	Difficulty	Currently doing start behavior?	OCD entangle-ment?	Can you deal with stop behavior temporarily?

Chart 10a

Brainstorming Possible Expectations and Limits (Example)

Start/ Desired behavior	Stop/ Undesirable behavior	Rank of importance of start behavior for the good of the child	Difficulty	Currently doing start behavior?	OCD entangle-ment?	Can you deal with stop behavior temporarily?
Doing therapy homework	Avoiding therapy homework	1	Varies	No	Yes	Yes
Going to school	Avoiding school	4	5–9	Yes	Sometimes	Yes
Doing schoolwork independently	Requiring excessive help or avoiding schoolwork	5	9	No	Sometimes	Yes
Getting up independently	Not getting up until yelled at	6	8	No	No	No
Going to bed at 9:00 P.M.	Keeping an irregular sleep schedule	2	9	Yes	Sometimes	Yes
Keeping regular mealtimes	Keeping irregular mealtimes	2	2	No	No	Yes
Moving reasonably quickly in A.M.	Excessive slowness in A.M. due to rituals	7	8	Yes	Yes, definitely	Yes, but not missing bus
Practicing musical instrument	Not practicing	8	5	Yes	No	Yes
Doing household chores	Not doing chores	9	Varies	Yes	Sometimes	Yes
Self-imposed time-outs; breathing exercises; constructive problem solving	Yelling, hitting, and breaking things	3	Varies; 5–10	Yes	Sometimes	No

Chart 10b

In general, those behaviors with a high importance ranking should be targeted first. Behaviors that are severely entangled with OCD should be forestalled until they are addressed in therapy. Start behaviors that have been observed, however infrequently, should be selected before ones that have never been seen, because the child has already demonstrated that he or she has the necessary skills to do the start behavior. Urging your child to attempt more than one difficult start behavior at a time should be avoided, because the endeavor is likely to seem overwhelming to the child and may not be attempted. Finally, only target one or two start behaviors at a time, especially for your child with OCD. Remember, each child is presumably selecting an important goal each week. For your child with OCD, these goals will usually be to do his or her therapy homework. You do not want other expectations to become more important than the therapy work. This necessarily means that until your child begins making significant progress in therapy, you will probably need to let go of many of the other expectations on your list.

Stop behaviors that you absolutely cannot deal with should have consequences even if you are not going to immediately target the associated start behavior as a goal. When goals are selected in this way, some parents respond, "But what about *x* behavior? It's not okay with me if my child does that!" Clearly, some behaviors, such as violence and destructive behaviors, are simply not acceptable. These are probably at least some of the behaviors that you indicated you absolutely cannot deal with. However, violent actions are clearly more important to address than destructive behavior. Does this mean you should ignore it if your child deliberately breaks things? No. Destructive behavior should always trigger a consequence. However, the importance of changing this behavior is lower and so the accompanying start behavior should not necessarily be a target that is encouraged, attended to, and tied to rewards right away. Because you are not targeting the start behavior and are not "expecting" it, you may be more able to manage your distress if the unacceptable behavior occurs. And, you will be more able to unemotionally enforce the consequence.

What about all the other behaviors that you don't want to see but can tolerate, at least temporarily? If the behavior is not dangerous or destructive and you can deal with it (such as yelling, mouthing off, or leaving belongings everywhere), then for now ignore the behavior you don't want, and if on the off chance you observe the related desired behavior, praise the child. Remember, the more issues you get upset about, the more you will engage in nagging or hostile behavior, diminishing your effectiveness. So, for now, if you can, let go of your expectation that these "bad" behaviors shouldn't occur, and keep your priorities in focus. This strategy does not mean that you will never target related start behaviors. It does mean that you will introduce them gradually as your child progresses. Remember, you are attempting to set expectations and limits in a way that will maximize your child's success.

Using the Brainstorming Possible Expectations and Limits worksheet that you completed earlier and the guidelines listed above, now complete the Setting Expectations and Limits worksheet. As usual, make copies first because you will use this form again. First, select a maximum of two start behaviors for your child to work on. Next, write the accompanying stop behaviors on the worksheet. List rewards for the start behaviors and logical and reasonable consequences or time-outs for the two stop behaviors. In addition, write down consequences for other stop behaviors that are ranked very important or that you cannot tolerate, which you will write in the Limits category. The rest of the stop behaviors on the Brainstorming sheet should fall in the Temporarily Ignored category.

For behaviors that are sometimes entangled with OCD, you will need to judge whether or not each behavior is more tolerable if it occurs because of the OCD. If it seems to you that the behavior is unacceptable if it is not related to OCD but is tolerable or excusable when it is OCD related, then the behavior will need to be listed in both the Limits category, with a specified consequence, and in the Temporarily Ignored category.

Whenever you have observed success with the current target start behaviors for a two- to three-week period, the behavior can be considered "mastered" and it is reasonable to expect it as a matter of course. However, to ensure that these behaviors continue, be sure to continually acknowledge and praise them. Your child is still displaying effortful behavior, and that deserves appreciation. When your child has mastered those two target start behaviors, he or she is probably ready to move on to the next ones on the list, and so it is time to start a new Setting Expectations and Limits worksheet. When you complete a new worksheet, you will select new target start behaviors for your child to begin working on. You will most likely select your target behaviors first from the other important or objectionable behaviors for which you have already identified consequences.

As the items in the Limits category are addressed and mastered, you will be able to move items from the Temporarily Ignored category up to the Limits category. Whenever you move an item into the Limits category, you need to find a natural or logical consequence or impose time-out to discourage the stop behavior. Similarly, for each new target start behavior that you identify, determine a tangible reward for completing the start behavior and keep in place whatever consequences you have already identified for the related stop behavior.

Determining What Is OCD and What Is "Bad" Behavior

By now, you have probably come up against this major hurdle. Some of your expectations and limits are likely entangled in OCD. You probably have written the word "sometimes" in the OCD entanglement column of the Brainstorming Possible Expectations and Limits worksheet. You know that sometimes your child displays undesirable behavior because of distress triggered by OCD. You're also sure that there are many times that the OCD isn't involved and your child could do the desired start behavior. Then there are those times when you aren't sure. So how do you approach these "sometimes" behaviors?

Unfortunately, how to deal with these behaviors is a judgment call on your part. So, what should you consider before you make your judgment? First, as we discussed earlier in this chapter, if it is a behavior that you absolutely cannot abide, OCD related or not, then you need to enforce the limit you have set. For the other, more tolerable behaviors, start

Setting Expectations and Limits

Target Start Behaviors (New Expectations)

Target #	Start/ Desired behavior	Stop/ Undesirable behavior	Reward for start behavior	Consequence for stop behavior
1				
2				

Limits on Other Stop Behaviors

	Stop/undesirable behavior	Consequence for stop behavior

Chart 10c

Setting Expectations and Limits

Stop Behaviors to Be Temporarily Ignored or Allowed

Chart 10c—continued

Setting Expectations and Limits Exercise

Target Start Behaviors (New Expectations)

Target #	Start/ Desired behavior	Stop/ Undesirable behavior	Reward for start behavior	Consequence for stop behavior
1	Self-imposed time-outs, breathing exercises, constructive problem solving	Hitting, kicking when angry	Star toward identified reward at each occurrence	Time-out or early bedtime (logical consequence—assume lack of behavioral control is due to fatigue)
2	Doing therapy work	Avoiding therapy work	½ hour video time	No extra video time

Limits on Other Stop Behaviors

	Stop/undesirable behavior	Consequence for stop behavior
1	Irregular mealtimes	Needs to eat with family; if a meal is missed, the kitchen is closed (logical consequence)
2	Irregular bedtimes	Assume he or she has too many obligations; begin to reduce or limit time-consuming activities (logical consequence)
3	Breaking things when angry	Replaces other people's broken things; makes do without own broken things (logical consequence)
4	Missing bus	Walks to school (natural consequence)
5	Waiting until yelled at to get out of bed	Receives two wake-up calls, then is ignored (limit then natural consequence)
6	Staying home from school because "sick"	Stays in bed when home from school sick; without TV, games, videos, etc. (logical consequence)

Chart 10d

Setting Expectations and Limits Exercise
(continued)

	Stop Behaviors to Be Temporarily Ignored or Allowed
1	Requiring excessive help to complete homework
2	Avoiding homework
3	Slowness in morning
4	Not doing chores
5	Yelling
6	Not practicing violin

Chart 10d—*continued*

by using your best guess to determine whether the behavior is driven by OC symptoms. When you notice the behavior, ask your child if it happened for some reason related to OCD. If your child confirms your hunch, and the behavior does not seem too important to you, find a way to temporarily accommodate the behavior.

However, be sure to discuss your quandary and your action with your child's therapist as soon as possible, for two reasons. First, some accommodations are such powerful reinforcers (e.g., school avoidance) that they can make the problem worse and therefore the unwanted behavior should never be permitted without some consequence. Quickly consulting with your child's therapist will prevent you from continuing to make temporary accommodations that are potentially damaging for very long. Second, your child's therapist will need to know about the problem so that it can be incorporated into the treatment hierarchy. If the child indicates that the behavior was not related to OCD, then use whatever consequence that you have already identified.

This strategy encourages your child to identify and own up to problems that he or she might otherwise want to hide. It also enables you to be flexible when OC problems arise, which feels better than punishing the child for a problem you feel he or she is not yet able to handle. And informing the therapist also ensures that the flexibility you permit will not last indefinitely, which would contribute to enabling your child's OCD. Once the trigger situation is added to the hierarchy, you know that your child will eventually work on the problem and then you will be able to place a limit on the behavior more consistently.

Some parents balk at this strategy because they believe their child will "milk" the OCD in order to win more sympathy and flexibility from the parents. If this is your concern, know that once your child's therapist begins to focus on the problem situation, many days of homework will be devoted to just this problem. The additional work will make the initial flexibility seem less desirable to the child, a consequence that will encourage better choices in the future.

Handling OC Moments

It's quite common for children and adults with OCD to agree to something in a non-OC moment, then resort to avoidance or find it quite difficult to resist their rituals when the trigger situation arises. Be prepared for this problem by developing a plan of action. How will you respond to pleas for reassurance or participation in rituals? Will you refuse to provide the desired reassurance or accommodation? If so, your child may become angry and fight engaging in the start behavior. Some children just need a little coaching in these situations. The following tips may help you through the tough times:

◊ **Externalize the problem.** "Is this the OCD bully talking?" "Who's in charge here, the bully or you?" "Do you really want to let the bully push you around this way?"

◊ **Empathize with your child's difficulty and validate the struggle.** "I know this is hard." "I understand that you feel you can't do this." "I know you can do it; you've beaten the bully before. You know that bully is just trying to psych you out." "I'm sorry it feels so bad. You know it won't feel bad for very long and then you'll feel great. You don't really want to feed the bully by letting it win."

◊ **Express confidence in your child's strength.** "I think you can win this one." "Come on, give it your best shot, take the risk. I'm here to support you." "I think you're strong enough to try this one."

◊ **Remind your child of previous successes.** "You've beaten the bully in harder situations than this one. Remember when you …"

◊ **Remind your child of his or her goals.** "You really want to be able to play soccer eventually. This is just one step along the way." "Remember what you're fighting for. It's worth it."

◊ **Remind your child that the OCD's main weapon is predicting failure.** "I think you're letting the bully psych you out. How can we boss it back?"

◊ **Remind your child of the consequence of not fighting.** "Do you really want to feed the bully by doing what it wants?" "Do you really want to make the bully stronger?"

◊ **Remind your child that when people fight back against OCD, the anxiety is temporary and they feel victorious.** "I know this feels terrible, but every time you fight back you find out the pain doesn't last very long and you feel terrific afterward."

For some children, and some moments, these reminders will do the trick. For others the persisting demands, anger, and anxiety will escalate. In these circumstances, you must stick to the plan agreed upon in the family meetings. Say, "I'm sorry this is so hard, but I'm your team member and my job right now is to say no to the bully (OCD)." "Even if you feel you can't fight this one, it's my job to fight it for you. I know you don't want me to right now, but when you were thinking more clearly this is what you wanted." These are moments when you have to be willing to experience the anxiety and distress of ritual prevention, when you have to absorb it without giving in to OCD's demands.

Sometimes, sticking to the plan seems impossible. Our answer to this is to attempt to be prepared with a backup plan that would prevent accommodating the OCD bully's demands. Roberto's and Brenda's families offer good examples of advance planning.

Eleven-year-old Roberto experienced obsessions related to accidents and harm coming to himself and others. In the past, his fears had prevented his family from traveling to visit out-of-state relatives. After working with a therapist and his family for some time, he agreed that he could travel and was willing to undertake this activity. His parents feared that, when they arrived at the airport, he would change his mind, have a tantrum in the airport, and insist that they return home. They didn't want to deal with a public tantrum because they worried that the airport personnel would not allow them on the plane if their child was too visibly upset. Naturally, they were reluctant to buy tickets that might not be used.

Sixteen-year-old Brenda was about to be released from a partial hospital treatment program. Her therapists felt that she was ready to return to school on a part-time basis. Brenda reluctantly agreed. Her mother believed that when the morning to start arrived, however, she would resist. In the past, her mother was instrumental in helping her feel okay. She knew her daughter would turn to her for excessive reassurance and help. Brenda's mother's job was in jeopardy because of her frequent absences from work. She needed to get to work on time, and she was concerned that her need to get to work would force her to relent.

In these cases it was important for the parents to have a backup strategy that would make it clear to their children that they would be following through with their agreed-upon plan. Roberto's parents identified a friend who would be willing to baby-sit their child for the duration of the vacation, just in case. They briefed this friend on the basics of taking care of their child and how to respond to some of his more difficult problems, and they requested that this friend accompany them to the airport. They made it clear to Roberto that the family would be going on a vacation to visit the grandparents, with or without him. He could choose to fight the OCD and take the risk of going on the flight, or he could stay with their friend, whom Roberto did not know very well. When the dreaded day arrived, Roberto was very distressed but he held it together. He really didn't want to have to spend a week with someone he didn't know very well. The family made it onto the plane without a hitch.

Brenda's mother devised a similar plan. She talked to people at work, church, and local nursing schools. She finally identified a trustworthy, retired schoolteacher who was the husband of a good friend. This man was willing to come to their house at a designated time. He was instructed as to what support would and would not be helpful to Brenda's recovery. The message to Brenda was that, either way, Mom was going to work. If Brenda felt stuck, then she would have to rely on the help of this man, who would not provide her with the kind of support that she had been used to. This backup plan allowed the mother the peace of mind to resist the pull of old patterns. She managed to save her job, and Brenda managed to get to school.

In this chapter we have reviewed and adapted parenting skills to increase your effectiveness with your child with OCD, because we believe your role as loving parent is key to your child's success. We have provided strategies that you can use to address issues commonly facing parents with children with OCD. Right now, reestablishing your parenting practices may seem daunting. As always, we encourage you to make changes one small methodical step at a time. We believe you will find the benefit well worth the effort.

Chapter 11

Finding Where You Fit In

One of the major hurdles of parenting any special-needs child is avoiding burnout. When people are confronted by a major problem, their immediate response is often to make that problem the number one priority and to sacrifice whatever is necessary to solve it. This may seem right to you. However, while that approach may carry you through a sprint, it will not work for a marathon. Helping your child with OCD is a long-term process, a marathon. If you routinely sacrifice your own needs, eventually you'll have nothing left to offer your child.

Success requires that you find a place for yourself in this process, that you replenish your resources as you draw from them, which necessitates self-care. To strike the proper balance between helping your child and caring for yourself, you will need to let go of beliefs that interfere with self-care, let go of perfectionism, and pace yourself. The attitudes toward yourself that will help you most are gentleness and compassion.

The barometer for whether or not you are maintaining balance is your own emotional well-being. If you are feeling chronically exhausted, irritable, resentful, empty, demoralized, hopeless, or overwhelmed, then you are not succeeding at maintaining balance. Such feelings scream, "You cannot continue this way." If these feelings are extreme, you may need to consider getting professional help. At a minimum, you must step back and revamp your strategy. Doing more of the same will only guarantee that your resources will be depleted further.

We don't want to put more on your to-do list, but now is the time to begin taking care of yourself. Let's briefly review the kinds of self-care activities and attitudes that should be part of your lifestyle. You will not be able to follow all of these recommendations all of the time. What's important is that you consistently make efforts to care for yourself.

- ◊ **Sleep approximately eight hours per night.** This is the average sleep requirement of adults. Consistently getting less than eight hours of sleep makes you more vulnerable to stress and will invite problems related to sleep deprivation, such as fatigue, poor concentration, memory loss, learning and attention problems, and depression.

- ◊ **Eat well-balanced meals.** When people are stressed their junk-food intake (coffee, chips, chocolate) can go up and healthy food consumption can go down. Poor nutrition wears the body down, so curb your impulses and eat balanced meals with the family. Keep your caffeine consumption to reasonable levels.

- ◊ **Curb other unhealthy habits.** Caretakers can fall victim to overusing alcohol when stressed. Similarly, when stressed, smokers tend to increase their nicotine use, worsening the ill effects of that habit. While such behaviors may appear to promote relaxation when use is occasional or moderate, overuse exacerbates depressive and anxious feelings. If you routinely consume more than two drinks a day, you are probably adding to your stress rather than lessening it.

- ◊ **Stick with an exercise program.** Cardiovascular exercise helps combat the physiological effects of stress and makes your system more resilient. It's also a strong antidepressant in and of itself. Strive for a minimum of twenty minutes of exercise three times a week. Consult with your doctor before beginning. Start with lighter, gentler activities such as walking, and increase the intensity as you build up strength.

- ◊ **Take time to relax every day.** Stressed minds are stuck on the "on" setting. You need to engage in an activity that helps you turn off deliberate thought. During your relaxation activity you must suspend problem solving. If thoughts tempt you to ruminate, let go of them and refocus on your breathing or body sensations. Activities that promote relaxation include meditation, massage, yoga, bubble baths, prayer, and music. Relaxation exercises are frequently taught by cognitive behavioral therapists and recordings on tapes or CDs can also be bought from bookstores.

◊ **Embrace fun activities in your life.** Find and do whatever nurtures your spirit. There is nothing that can refresh quite so effectively as a good laugh or a good time. Just be careful not to choose activities that will heap additional responsibilities on you.

◊ **Protect your sense of identity.** Keep your toe in the work world or in some other nonfamily activity. Functioning in this outside environment will help to remind you that you are more than just your child's mom or dad.

◊ **Work against becoming isolated; keep friends in your life.** This is key for two reasons. You need people to talk to for emotional support. And you need people you can call on for practical help if circumstances become difficult.

◊ **Be your own cheerleader.** A simple step to reducing stress is to learn to appreciate your efforts and own your victories. Tearing yourself down at every opportunity only demoralizes you. Consistently noticing what is right about your efforts will encourage you just as it does your children.

◊ **Live in the present.** The key to living in the present is to accept that bad things may happen that are outside of your control. Instead of worrying about these events that you can't control, work toward outcomes that are within your control. Decide to deal with the problems at hand rather than attempting to anticipate every bump or pothole. Lastly, let go and forgive when problems are resolved.

Chances are that the suggestions above are not new to you. So if you are not caring for yourself the cause probably isn't not knowing what to do; it probably comes down to some other thinking or feeling obstacle. Take a moment to think about what it would mean to you to actually follow these recommendations regularly. What thoughts pop into your head? Write them down below.

_____

_____

_____

_____

Obstacles to a Parent's Self-Care

Next, we will discuss some common obstacles to self-care that parents encounter. After you have finished this chapter, return to the thoughts you've written down. If they still make sense to you, revisit the challenging questions in chapter 7 and use them as a model for questions to challenge your problematic beliefs in this situation.

"No Time"

One of the biggest barriers to self-care is the chronic lament "No time. No time. No time." If you don't have enough time, then your standards are probably too high (you expect too much of yourself) or you're trying to do too much. You are not picking and choosing. Instead, you consistently add more to your to-do list.

We have talked before about the cost of a priority: making something a priority means that you're willing to let other things slide or go undone to ensure that the priority receives enough attention. Making self-care a priority means you have to let go of perfectionist standards. Everything can't get done and everything can't be done right. Doing fewer things and doing them less perfectly accomplishes two things: it reduces stress—you're no longer striving for impossible standards—and it creates time—time you use for basic self-care.

In chapter 7, we encouraged you to make a list of priorities and to eliminate some of the tasks that you routinely do, such as housecleaning, carpooling, paying bills, doing laundry, performing volunteer work, and grocery shopping. If you did so and you are still feeling overwhelmed, then it is time to revisit that list. We have created a Task Priorities worksheet for you to complete that will help you to drop activities, find alternatives, and find ways to lower your standards. List your tasks. Indicate that a task is essential with an *E,* nonessential with an *N,* or done to too high a standard with an *H.* In the last column write a new plan for each task: no change, do it to a lower standard, have it done by another person, or eliminate the task completely.

"No One Will Understand"

Believing that "other people don't have problems" and "no one will understand" can prevent parents from reaching out to old and new friends. Related to these beliefs is the prediction "People will judge me, my child, or my family."

If you find yourself accepting these beliefs, ask yourself, "Who are these people? What makes their opinion matter?" Sure, there are people who won't understand or who will judge. However, there are also people who will understand, won't judge, and will want to help. You need *those* people in your life. If you never reach out, you won't ever find them. When you run into the ignorant, judgmental, unhelpful sort (and you probably will), don't give up, just toss those fish back, and say, "Next!"

The price you pay for good friends is the disappointment you experience in the search for them. Supportive friends are well worth this price. If you can't find supportive people in your family, neighborhood, or religious organization, then try joining a support group. If you can't find groups in your area, turn to your computer. There are wonderful people available through online support groups.

Task Priorities

Task	Priority Status	New Plan

Chart 11a

"My Needs Don't Count"

By far the biggest obstacles to self-care that Dr. Fitzgibbons sees in parents in her practice are the following ideas:

- ◇ My parents would not have put themselves first.

- ◇ I have no extra time because it's all going to other family members.

- ◇ I'm not the priority right now.

- ◇ Parents are supposed to sacrifice for their children.

- ◇ Children come first.

- ◇ I'm strong so I should just hang in there and do without.

- ◇ I don't need as much as my child.

- ◇ What I want is not important.

- ◇ The neediest person should get the most.

- ◇ It doesn't matter whether I get sleep.

- ◇ My life and friends do not matter right now.

- ◇ Parents should only take what's left over.

It's very hard to dispute these statements because in many ways the ideas expressed are absolutely right. Raising children does require sacrifice and putting children's needs first, and even more so when resources (time and money) are limited.

The problem with these thoughts is that for the most part they are too rigid and too black-and-white. It's as if you can make only one choice, give either to your child *or* to yourself. If you really only had *one* choice, then you would be right to choose your child over yourself. But we are not talking about one choice; we're talking about many choices that come up multiple times a day. And because these choices present themselves so often, you do have the opportunity to meet your child's needs some of the time and your own some of the time.

When you take each choice separately, sometimes your child's need will be more important and you'll want to spend the resources there. Other times you will find that your needs are at least as important as your child's. When that happens, creating balance means that you allocate resources to yourself. If you don't see each choice as separate, you'll never be able to carve out the time you need to replenish yourself because you'll always automatically funnel your resources to your family.

It's hard to make choices in which we put ourselves first, even occasionally, because the messages we tell ourselves lead to our feeling selfish, and that feels bad. The problem is that those messages don't take into account that this is a long-term problem. Consider the following: You could take thirty minutes a day for a bubble bath, go to the gym three times a week, and occasionally see a movie with a friend, and manage to really be there for your family the rest of the time. Alternatively, you could never take any time for yourself and always put your family first; eventually you'd feel so exhausted and depressed that you wouldn't have the energy to meet the inevitable challenges and be truly supportive. You'd probably be angry and irritable, adding to all the family problems. In the long run, which scenario sounds more "selfish" to you?

In addition to your role as caregiver, you are a model for your children. As a parent, you're teaching your children how to parent and how to live by your example. Modeling consistent self-sacrifice sets up one of two possible outcomes for children when they grow up. For the child who follows in your footsteps, because your example is impossibly hard, he or she can feel guilty and selfish if he or she fails or depressed and burned out if he or she succeeds. Then there is the child who doesn't follow your lead, but instead learns that other people should always sacrifice everything to fulfill his or her needs. Such a child will surely make a very selfish and probably unhappy adult. Are these the outcomes you really want?

Learning to care for yourself will be a process in and of itself. There are a few points you'll need to understand about this process. First, finding balance often requires going to extremes. It's likely you have been living one extreme for some time, always putting everyone else's needs before your own. If this is the case, you will need to take steps toward the other extreme, putting yourself first too much. By doing so and allowing yourself to feel lazy and selfish, you'll become more accustomed to these feelings. As a result they'll hold less power over you, and you'll dismiss them more easily. Then you'll be better positioned to discover where a real balance lies.

Second, even if you change how you think about self-care, those feelings of selfishness or laziness may not go away until you learn to accept them. As long as you are invested in *not* feeling selfish or lazy, you are damning yourself to have those feelings. Paradoxically, those feelings are inescapable when you want to escape them because, as you might tell yourself, "there is always more I *could* do if only I wasn't so selfish or lazy."

Just as your child needs to accept anxiety to conquer it, you will need to accept feeling selfish and lazy in order to be free of those feelings. Your best bet is to accept them as part of the process. Remember, changing habits often requires feeling uncomfortable. The more you behave differently, the more likely it is that you'll begin to think and feel differently. To get yourself over the hump, keep reminding yourself that you'll be no good to your child unless you learn to balance your own needs with the needs of your family.

We hope this chapter has helped you to recognize the importance of self-care and to rethink some of your beliefs that may have interfered with creating balance between your needs and the needs of family members. As with all of the work you have already begun, these changes will probably not come easily but if you steadily persist while showing compassion for yourself, you will undoubtedly reap the benefits. Now we turn our attention to your role in regard to your child's school.

Chapter 12

Parenting and the School

Children spend almost as many waking hours at school as they do at home. A few children with OCD manage to get through the school day without apparent OCD symptoms. Most likely, they are keeping their obsessive thoughts secret, waiting until they get home, where it is safe, to engage in their compulsive behaviors. Others perform rituals at school, leaving teachers and fellow students to wonder about their unusual behaviors.

Team Support at School

You may be tempted to not tell your child's teachers and other school personnel about the OCD. If you choose that course, they will form their own opinions about your child's rituals, anxiety, apparent daydreaming, unfinished schoolwork, or frequent bathroom trips. Even if your child doesn't exhibit OCD symptoms at school now, that may change as symptoms change.

School districts vary in the ways they handle children with special needs. Start by discussing the issue with your child and the rest of the mental health care team—his or her doctors and therapist. We advise being open and clear with your child about how much you are telling people about the OCD. Provide written information about OCD to teachers and other school personnel who may be involved, such as the school psychologist, counselor, or nurse. The booklets *Obsessive-Compulsive Disorder in Children and Adolescents: A Guide,* by Hugh Johnston and J. Jay Fruehling (2002), and *School Personnel: A Critical Link in the Identification, Treatment, and Management of OCD in Children and Adolescents,* by Gail B. Adams, Ed.D., and Marcia Torchia, RN (1998), are inexpensive resources available through the Obsessive-Compulsive Foundation (OCF). *Teaching the Tiger* by Marilyn P. Dornbush, Ph.D., and Sheryl K. Pruitt, M.Ed. (1993), is a bit more expensive, but it is a very good resource for school personnel involved in teaching children and adolescents with OCD, attention deficit hyperactivity disorder, and Tourette's syndrome. The OCF also makes available an educator awareness and training module designed to teach professionals and parents of school-age children with OCD. This package contains two videos and four booklets, entitled "How to Recognize and Respond to OCD in School-Age Children."

Don't be critical if there is a lack of knowledge about OCD within your school district. This lack of knowledge is not uncommon. Treat school personnel with acceptance and embrace them as new members of your child's recovery team, not as adversaries. You may even be able to find resources in your community, such as the local affiliate of the OCF or National Alliance for the Mentally Ill (NAMI), that could provide an in-service presentation about OCD at your child's school.

Set up a communication system between yourself, your child's teacher and/or school counselor, and, if possible, your child's therapist. Progress updates can be giving in meetings between you, the teacher, and your child and in private meetings between you and the teacher. Weekly or biweekly phone calls or e-mails will also be helpful. Let the teacher or other school personnel know specifically what developments you would like to be made aware of, such as medication side effects or progress of OCD symptoms. Know that your child's therapist may include the school setting in some of your child's E/RP exercises. Be careful, however, to make sure that a well-meaning teacher doesn't take the lead in the exercises—it can be tempting for a teacher or other support person to become an amateur behavior therapist in his or her zeal to help a child. Communicating frequently and being open to the teacher's concerns and suggestions will help prevent this.

Lobby for all the accommodations your child needs and help the teachers understand why they are needed. Then, as your child progresses in his or her treatment, set up a systematic program for gradually withdrawing the accommodations. Your child and the therapist will need to be involved in planning this program.

Helping Your Child Face OCD Challenges at School

As your child's teacher learns more about OCD, the behavior will become more understandable to him or her. The teacher's anger, frustration, or worry will likely be replaced with acceptance, concern, and a willingness to be a part of your child's support team. Children with OCD sometimes appear inattentive or distracted when they are having intrusive thoughts and worries or silently counting, praying, or engaging in other rituals. Some are even misdiagnosed with attention deficit hyperactivity disorder (ADHD). It's not uncommon for OCD to coexist with ADHD, however, so don't assume that a diagnosis of OCD means your child doesn't have ADHD.

Often, adults and children with OCD suffer silently and secretly with anxiety and fear. When they're fighting the compulsions, the stress can be overwhelming. Help teachers arrange "safe" places and people at school. Giving a discreet signal, your child can slip away to this area or seek out one of these staff members when the stress or anxiety gets to be too much.

Teasing is a problem for many children, especially if their manifestation of OCD makes them appear a bit different. Teachers can help prevent teasing by instructing the class about health problems, such as asthma, diabetes, ADHD, depression, OCD, and others. It is generally best for a teacher not to single out a child with OCD or another specific disorder. Providing information about all kinds of problems helps children understand that we all have problems and that OCD is just one of many.

Worries about contamination can make a day at school feel like an obstacle course for a child with OCD. Negotiating halls without touching the wrong things or people can make a child late for class. Frequent hand washing means numerous trips to the bathroom. If accommodating these needs is necessary, you, your child, and his or her therapist need to decide how much and for how long. At first, your child may need to be allowed to avoid certain items or people, be late for classes, or make frequent trips to the bathroom. This should be done without drawing undue attention. Then, as CBT progresses, accommodation can be gradually reduced. The teacher might give a certain number of bathroom or hall passes each day and then gradually and discreetly reduce the number offered per day, and then per week.

Reassurance seeking is a common problem for children with OCD. These compulsions are often masked as ordinary questions or concerns about assignments or activities. Children with OCD may ask the same question repeatedly, rephrasing it slightly each time. Children might even seem to be clowning around or trying to cause trouble. When teachers recognize the questions as compulsions, they can privately discuss the problem with the child, and together they can come up with solutions for handling them. They might limit the number of questions each day or regarding each assignment, then gradually reduce the limit.

Test taking, writing, and reading can take longer or be fraught with anxiety for children with OCD. Again, insist that accommodations be made by the school to allow the child some flexibility, but only when necessary and for as long as necessary. Your child needs to understand that recovery depends on facing challenges whenever possible, and teachers need to understand that some accommodations are going to be essential during the recovery process. Work with teachers to come up with creative and *temporary* solutions. Below are some ideas:

◆ reducing the workload for the child with OCD

◊   giving extra time for completing assignments and tests

◊   allowing check marks to be used on tests instead of boxes to be filled in

◊   permitting typed or computer-generated homework instead of handwritten work for children with writing compulsions

◊   letting the child work with another student or with a tutor

◊   allowing the child to tape-record lectures instead of taking notes

◊   providing a quiet place at school for taking tests or studying

The Special Education Option

Children with severe OCD or OCD that is complicated with learning disabilities or other disorders may need special education services. Your child may qualify as "seriously emotionally disturbed" (SED) under the Individuals with Disabilities Education Act (IDEA) if an evaluation finds one or more of the following:

◊   an inability to learn

◊   an inability to build or maintain satisfactory interpersonal relationships

◊   inappropriate types of behavior or feelings under normal circumstances

◊   general pervasive mood of unhappiness or depression

◊   a tendency to develop physical symptoms or fears associated with personal or school problems

Another alternative is to classify OCD with other neurobiological disorders under the "other health impaired" (OHI) category when applying for services under IDEA. Children who don't qualify for IDEA may qualify for special services under section 504 of the Rehabilitation Act of 1973 if physical or mental impairment substantially limits a major life activity, such as learning, working, or socializing. This option involves much less paperwork, but there may also be less parental involvement and less legal obligation for school personnel to carry out plans. If you think your child should be receiving special education, check out the Resources section. *Negotiating the Special Education Maze: A Guide for Parents and Teachers,* by Winifred Anderson, Stephen Chitwood, and Deidre Hayden (1997), and *The Complete IEP Guide: How to Advocate for Your Special Ed Child,* by Lawrence M. Siegel (2001), can introduce you to the basics of special education. You may also want to consult resources in your community, such as your local Parent-Teacher Association (PTA).

Chapter 13

Special Issues, and into the Future

We've covered many of the issues that parents of children with OCD will encounter, but there are a few issues we haven't yet addressed. What can parents do when a child refuses all treatment? How can parents promote the healing of family relationships? We'll explore the answers to these questions in this chapter. Finally we'll discuss how to promote your child's continued success in the future.

Children Who Refuse Treatment

Some children reject all treatment efforts. This is very difficult for parents because they see their child suffering and they feel helpless to do anything. While it may be true that you can't make your child participate in any treatment, it's probably not true that you're helpless. There are things that you can do. And although these things can't be guaranteed to change your child's position they will, in time, increase the odds that your child will come around.

The most important thing you can do is remain hopeful and confident that treatment can help. When you see your child struggling or suffering, remind him or her that treatment could help. Seven-year-old Julie's parents let her know that they were just waiting for a word from her to get her the help she needed. They didn't nag her about her refusal to go to the initial visit to the therapist they'd found, and they honored her decision. They continued to empathize with her as she suffered, but they made it clear that there was a way out if she wanted it. After four months, she consented to treatment, deciding it would be a good idea to check out the therapist. By the day of the first appointment, instead of dreading it she was looking forward to getting started. In the long run, Julie's parents probably saved several weeks of costly therapy time by waiting until Julie had decided that tackling her OCD was worth the risk.

Proceed with the family plan regardless of whether your child with OCD tackles goals to combat the OCD or focuses on other issues. Feel free to suggest appropriate OCD goals occasionally, but do not insist on them. Do continue to insist on growth goals for everyone. Establishing and keeping the process going, regardless of the child's involvement in CBT, creates the kind of family norm that encourages everyone to admit and work on personal problems. Eventually, this norm may lead the child to decide that it is okay to have a problem, making it seem safer to admit to and grapple with the OCD.

As we discussed in chapter 9, we highly recommend that you work with a cognitive behavioral therapist experienced in E/RP to establish a timeline for the removal of family rituals and family avoidances. Many children lack interest in treatment because the family is doing so much in the service of the disorder that having unmanaged OCD seems more doable than the treatment. Thus, when a child refuses treatment it's very important for family members to crawl out from under the OCD burden. Once a clear timeline has been ironed out during family meetings, stick to it. Remember to make steps *very* small. Never withdraw any family ritual or avoidance abruptly. Always give plenty of warnings alerting the child to what will be happening and when. Of course, the reluctant child may well find ways to avoid or ritualize further to compensate for the family's changed behavior. This can be difficult for family members to see, especially when it looks like the child's OCD is suddenly much worse, or when he or she is telling you that you're making it worse. Remember, enabling behaviors make the OCD stronger and prevent children from fully understanding their own difficulties and strengths. When the child carries the burden alone, the desire to fight back is more likely to emerge. Unfortunately, even with these tactics, there is no telling how long a child might persist in refusing treatment. Despite not knowing, you need to maintain a compassionate attitude and hold a steady course.

If your child has refused treatment because he or she doesn't like the professionals that you have found, keep looking for others. Sometimes, children don't want to work solely because they haven't felt connected to the professionals they have met. Eventually, you may luck out and find someone who clicks with your child. When that happens, your child may miraculously feel ready. Eight-year-old Tommy didn't feel comfortable with the therapist his parents had found, even though she was the most qualified child psychologist in town. She agreed with his parents that perhaps another therapist might reach him and recommended a colleague. The new therapist had less training and less experience, but Tommy took to him immediately and made rapid progress.

If you've taken all of the above steps, and your child continues to refuse treatment and is steadily declining, you may want to consider inpatient treatment or a boarding school that has experience with emotionally challenged children. An inpatient facility for adolescents is run by the Menninger OCD Treatment Center in Topeka, Kansas. As of this printing, there are no inpatient facilities specializing in treatment of younger children with OCD. Check with the Obsessive-Compulsive Foundation or your local OCF affiliate to find other facilities that provide OCD treatment and schools qualified to help. Sometimes temporary inpatient care at a mental health facility is necessary because the child is threatening harm to self or others. In such cases, safety will be your primary concern. Beyond that, try to find professionals within the facility who specialize in OCD, but do not be surprised if there are no experts. Take the hospitalization as an opportunity to regroup and find the best treatment possible after discharge.

Family Relationships

As we mentioned in chapters 3 and 9, family relationships can take a hard hit when a child's OCD is pushing the whole family around. Siblings can feel overlooked and resentful of the special treatment their sibling with OCD receives. Parents can turn against each other, wrongly assigning blame, sometimes feeling angry because of conflicts of opinion, sometimes feeling that the burden is shouldered inequitably. When a child begins to function better, much of this stress is lifted and the active conflict subsides. But the tendency to harbor grudges over harsh words spoken in anger and actions taken out of frustration is a common human trait. Grudges can create permanent distance and frostiness in relationships, sometimes permanently damaging a family. If they develop, they should be addressed once the OCD is weaker.

Some of the recommendations we have made work against this outcome, particularly for the siblings. The family meetings, by encouraging all members to make and work toward goals, ensure that siblings get their parents' attention and rewards for their work, making the situation more equal. The reinstatement of disciplinary strategies for your affected child that may have lapsed will also weaken a sibling's perception that the child with OCD gets away with too much. The goals we recommended in chapter 9, which promote estranged or angry family members actually spending time together, present an opportunity for reconnection once the OCD has weakened.

However, there is another important strategy that we have not yet discussed. This strategy is essential to preventing a rift between siblings from becoming a canyon: each parent needs to spend sufficient time with *every* child. The fifteen minutes of "YAMA time" (you and me alone time) each day recommended in chapter 10 is a good starting point. We recommend an additional hour per child on the weekends. During this time, you need to work to "hold" your child's negative feelings.

When you simply listen to your children talk without judging, arguing, or even commenting very much, you "hold" their feelings, communicating your acceptance. Your unaffected children are not saints; they cannot be expected to go through this difficult experience without having negative emotional reactions. Their resentful and angry feelings are normal and understandable. Your children need you to provide an accepting environment that permits them to acknowledge and deal with all of their feelings without fear of criticism or rejection. A safe environment allows them to deal with their feelings in a healthy way. Negative emotions that are denied because they seem wrong to the parent do not generally disappear but tend to fester and leak out in insidious and damaging ways. Such feelings fuel conflict and negative behavior, increasing stress and making life worse for everyone in the family.

As a parent, you can't force children to admit negative feelings or identify them. You can't force them to talk or open up. However, the more you listen without challenging them, correcting them, or trying to change them, the more likely it is that they will talk to you. When these feelings are "held" by a loving parent, children become more amenable to taking a rational perspective. As a result, painful feelings often either evaporate completely or at least seem less burdensome.

When the worst of the storm is over, everyone will need to assess the damage done to the family relationships. Much of the healing that will need to take place will necessitate some people letting go of guilt and others letting go of grudges. Time spent together wherein family members hear each other out without defense or counterattacks is essential. Individuals owning their hurtful actions and apologizing for wrongful acts is key. Active forgiveness and conciliatory actions are necessary. Parents and children alike need to participate in healing, because the rifts can run deep in these relationships. When attempts to listen, understand, apologize, and forgive do not work, seek help. Wounded families who try to go on without healing can become crippled, and that's not good for anyone's happiness or well-being.

Into the Future: Relapse Prevention

When your child is far along in treatment and you have witnessed remarkable gains and changes, you may think, "The problem is cured! We never have to deal with this again! Now we can go back to life as usual." It's a tempting and alluring thought. But it's wrong. Clinging to this belief will work against your child. As we discussed in chapter 6, it's important to let go of that "normal" dream because your wanting things to be normal will prevent you and your child from establishing a lifestyle that keeps the OCD weak and manageable. You and your child can never safely go back. This is a long-term problem that requires a long-term solution.

You probably want to argue, "But why? Obviously, my child is doing great!" To explain this, let us go back to an analogy we used early on to explain why E/RP works. The old OCD train track—where the child would feel distressed by obsessions, experience the obsessive thoughts frequently, and respond to the distress with avoidance and rituals— was never dismantled. *That train track is still there.* It's not gone because learning never disappears. It can be weakened and forgotten by practicing other behaviors and strengthening other thought and feeling patterns, but the old learning itself remains intact, lying there dormant, ready to be used again.

To understand this, think back to the algebra class you took during your freshman year of high school. You may have struggled with that class; it was so hard. Then when you finished you turned the book in and put it out of your mind, until that first college math class when you had to study algebra again. What you probably noticed was that you still had to study, but this time it was easier. You were relearning rather than learning for the first time. Whenever you go back to something that you have done before it's always easier than it was the first time because the learning never disappears. It's just sitting there waiting to be reactivated, like an old refrigerator, discarded and dusty, that just needs to be plugged in to work again.

Because your child learned the OC responses so thoroughly before treatment, he or she can never afford to go back to those behaviors because the old learning will reactivate. What's more, your child must actively live a lifestyle that continues to strengthen the new learning so that he or she doesn't inadvertently begin going down the old train track again.

Lifestyle Changes to Promote Relapse Prevention

It's important that your child continue to abstain from rituals. On the other hand, the child should not have to spend the rest of his or her life doing E/RP exercises for an hour or more per day. By the end of treatment, concentrated daily work will for the most part no longer be necessary and your child's lifestyle can begin to approach a more normal one. Remember, the goal of all the extreme E/RP treatment has been to bring the child's functioning into a more "normal" range. Unfortunately, people with OCD have a very difficult time judging what is "normal." Trying to do so can become a quagmire of uncertainty. Below are several ways you can help your child maintain progress and function at a more normal level.

Establish Rules to Live By

It can be helpful, when promoting a fairly normal lifestyle that guards against the likelihood of relapse, for a child to follow some fairly rigid rules. These rules approximate "normal" with a slight leaning toward exposure. Following these rules makes reverting to old rituals less likely. Not every affected child has to follow every rule; the rules that any particular child requires are determined by his or her original obsessive concerns.

1. Never wash for social convention and only wash for a maximum of twenty seconds.

2. Showers should not occur more than once per day and should not exceed ten minutes.

3. Only one check is ever okay, and only in circumstances where other people check also.

4. Only one question to verify information is okay. If the information is not clear after that, take the risk.

5. Do not apologize unless someone tells you he or she is hurt or angry without your asking. Never apologize more than once.

6. Prayers should not exceed ten minutes a day or should not exceed the cultural norm.

7. Do not collect anything. Throw out any item for which there is not an immediate use.

8. Do not engage in sentimental collecting. You can't afford it.

9. Never engage in any blatantly superstitious behavior (e.g., touching, tapping, repeating, counting, reciting magic phrases, and so on).

10. Always leave something out of order, and vary what that something is.

Avoid the "Normal" Trap

We are aware that there is a certain inconsistency in what we are saying. On the one hand, we say that the point of treatment is to help your child get within the normal range of functioning. On the other hand, we say that everyone must let go of the idea of normal. These two ideas seem to be at cross-purposes. This is really just another paradox of OCD. To get to normal, you have to let go of the dream of normal. The rules above approximate normal, but they are not normal both because normal people don't have to follow rigid rules and because normal people can do some of the things that the rules forbid.

After treatment most folks, adults and children, want to find ways that allow them to do their ritual to a small extent. They justify the behavior by comparing themselves to the people around them ("My mother would wash before she ate, so therefore I should be able to wash before I eat"). We call this the "normal" trap.

Unfortunately, this logic, comparing the desired behavior to other people's behavior to determine what is okay, misses the point of the problem. Normal people's actions are not an accurate gauge of what are and are not okay behaviors because normal people don't have any OCD consequences linked to their activities. The proper way to determine whether any potential activity is okay is to decide whether the action is so important, so necessary, that it is worth the risk of falling back into active OCD. Remember, every time the old responses are practiced, the old track is reactivated. "Normal" people do not have to deal with this. They can wash their hands and check their work with impunity. Not so for your child. When your child engages in washing and checking that a normal person would do, it can reactivate the old response patterns. Doing this enough can lead the child down the old track.

Consider the following scenario: You, your child, and I are standing outside my office. We are reading a note on the door that says, "Anthrax inside. Keep out." You, your child, and I are all alarmed and frightened by this information and so we do not go in. In fact, we leave the building. *We are all in agreement* that there is danger and we should leave. This is a normal behavior, a correct decision. However, this is where a normal person and your child differ.

The folks in the white suits come and clean up my office building. They give the "all clear" message. They tell me it's safe to return. So what do I do? I return to work in my previously contaminated office. What do you do? You make an appointment for your child to come back to see me. But the day of the appointment comes and what does your child do? Your child doesn't want to return. Isn't there another place we could meet? Isn't there a different building? Couldn't I come to the house? So even though your child initially made the correct "normal" decision, the old intolerance for uncertainty is reactivated. Suddenly the OCD is active again.

This is a tough lesson to learn. Doing something because it's normal comes with a price tag for the person with OCD. Sometimes, as in the case above, it's clearly the right choice to pay the price of possibly reactivating the OCD because there's real danger. But, most of the time, desired normal behaviors are not worth this price. So the question to use to evaluate whether a behavior is okay is not "What would a normal person do?" The question should be "Is the behavior so important, so necessary, in this circumstance that it's worth jeopardizing my recovery and having to fight OCD all over again?"

Set Up Ongoing Exposures

Incorporate regular E/RP exercises into your child's life, and fold these activities into family contracts. These exercises don't usually need to be done daily. They just need to be done often enough to keep the concerns weak. Start with once a month. (You don't want the exercises themselves to become rituals to ward off fears of relapse.)

Many children are dismayed to realize that they will always need to do E/RP exercises. Parents need to be prepared for this and help them to accept the necessity of ongoing E/RP work. However, when occasional E/RP exercises are done routinely it's really no big deal because the OCD is still weak. So whatever the hardest exposures were, encourage your child to do them again every once in a while, if they're easy. If they turn out to be not so easy, encourage the child to practice more until they become easy. For younger kids, keep those exposure games a part of your child's recreational repertoire. Fling spitballs at your child! Play catch with lint from the dryer! Play the games and do the activities used in treatment to keep the OCD weak. Sing the song that follows. This song was written by Kathy Parrish, M.A., M.S., of the Anxiety and Agoraphobia Treatment Center in Philadelphia, for a children's workshop that Dr. Fitzgibbons and Ms. Parrish conduct at the OCF's annual conference called the Kids' G.O.A.L. Support Group. This is a play group for young kids that warms them up to do E/RP throughout the conference weekend. The song is sung to the tune of "Row, Row, Row Your Boat."

Kid's G.O.A.L. Group Theme Song
By Kathy Parrish, M.A., M.S.

Touch, touch, touch the germs
Put them in your mouth
Every time you boss it back
Your OCD heads south.

Think, think, think bad thoughts
Make them even worse
Think the thoughts you fear the most
To break the OC curse!

Put, put, put, your hand
Put it on the potty
When you do what OC hates
You help yourself a lotty!

Up, up, up and down
The dreaded worry hill
But if you do your E/RP
Then you'll feel stronger still!

Print, print, print your letters
Sloppy as can be
Make your schoolwork look real bad
And you'll feel happy!

Don't, don't, don't repeat
Feel the fear and say
I can live my life just fine
Who needs you anyway!

Step, step, on the crack
Break your mother's back
Break the rules—it's really cool
And learn to just relax!

Feel, feel, feel the fear
And do it anyway
You'll win the fight, oh what a sight
You're stronger every day!

Just go have some fun
And let yourself be free
Take it from me—I should know
You can beat OC!

Help Your Child "Get a Life"

The best defense against relapse is having a full and meaningful life. For children, that means they are doing fun things, maintaining friendships, and developing skills that they value. As OCD recedes, help your children get back the activities and friendships that have slipped away.

Manage Stress

OCD has a tendency to resurface when people are stressed and feel the least able to deal with it. For that reason, it's important that your child master the skills to manage stress. All of the stress-reduction activities that we detailed for you are important for your child as well. Some parents think that this vulnerability to OCD during times of stress provides a reason to protect their child from all stressful situations. But avoiding stress would only deny the child many meaningful challenges that could boost confidence and self-esteem. Instead of protecting your child from stress, help your child practice balance in life.

Encourage Your Child to Weed the Garden

Your child's life is like a garden. It has good soil, so the garden can be very beautiful. Unfortunately, its good soil also makes it vulnerable to OCD weeds—fears and rituals. When these weeds are recognized early, they are easy to pull out using E/RP, and the garden remains beautiful. But if the weeds are left to flourish they take over and all the beauty is lost. The longer the weeds are ignored, the harder it is to reestablish the plants that are wanted. Help your child to spot the old, familiar weeds and new, unrecognized weeds. Encourage your child to pull these weeds out before they take hold.

Keep Holding Family Meetings

One of your best tools to keep your child's recovery on track is to continue the practice of holding family meetings until all children have left the nest. The practice of making weekly goals and conducting ongoing self-assessment will help keep your child on track and will help keep the family dynamics supportive of your child's recovery.

Take Slips in Stride

Understand that one of the biggest threats to a child's ability to maintain gains comes when a slip has occurred. When children have slipped, by avoiding something they know they should have confronted, or by ritualizing in a situation that they had mastered, they are vulnerable to thinking the game is lost. They can become so demoralized that they don't care about trying anymore. Let your child know that slips happen to everyone. The falling down is not the important problem; what's important is getting up after a fall and trying again. All is not lost unless effort stops. Remind your child that learning is *never* erased. If he or she has created a new track but is suddenly chugging along on the old OCD line, he or she only has to jump back to that new track. It is still there. There is no need to create a whole new one. As long as slips are treated as a normal problem that can be solved with courage and perseverance, your child will be empowered to fight again.

Conclusion

When you began to read this book, you may not have known whether your child was struggling with OCD. You may not have known what treatments are available, and you probably felt helpless and at a loss about what to do to help your child. The most important goal of this book has been to help you feel hopeful rather than helpless. It's natural to feel helpless when you don't know what to do. That's why we have done our best to equip you with tools that will help.

From the beginning, we have wrestled with the conflict between our knowledge that many parents reading this book would want to "fix" their child themselves and our strong belief that taking on such a role undermines the more important role of being a parent. So we have tried to provide you with a road map for helping that preserves and strengthens your primary parental role. The most important part of the plan we've offered you is to help you create a family environment where all individuals own and address their own problems or growth needs. In creating this new norm for your family, you are changing your family in a way that will support your child's personal battle against OCD. Your child's ownership of the problem will remain intact, yet he or she will also feel supported by others since other family members are also working on important personal goals. Lastly, hard work will be recognized and rewarded as a matter of course.

Throughout this process our goal has been to keep you, the parent, in focus. This book is for you. Yes, it is meant to help you help your child. However, a key aspect of this process is not losing sight of yourself as your family's needs threaten to engulf you. By keeping you in focus, we hope that you will remember how very important it is that you protect and nurture yourself. When parents run on empty, the car just won't go. These have been our aims. We appreciate your hard work in reading this book and your attempts to implement a plan to assist your child's recovery.

Resources

For Children and Teens

Foster, Constance H. 1997. *Kids Like Me.* Ellsworth, Maine: Dilligaf Publishing.

Heyman, Isobel, and Ian Frampton. 2000. *Why Me? Obsessive-Compulsive Disorder: Information for Young People, Families, and Professionals.* London: Institute of Psychiatry at the Maudsley, King's College London; The Wellcome Trust; and Line TV Ltd. CD-ROM (Available through Obsessive Action; see Organizations, below.)

Moritz, E. Katia, and Jennifer Jablonsky. 1998. *Blink, Blink, Clop, Clop: Why Do We Do Things We Can't Stop? An OCD Storybook.* Secaucus, N.J.: Childswork/Childsplay, LLC.

Wagner Aureen, Pinto. 2000. *Up and Down the Worry Hill: A Children's Book about Obsessive-Compulsive Disorder and Its Treatment.* Rochester, N.Y.: Lighthouse Press, Inc.

Wever, Chris. 1994. *The Secret Problem.* Concord West, NSW, Australia: Shrink-Rap Press.

For Parents

Anderson, Winifred, Stephen Chitwood, and Deidre Hayden. 1997. *Negotiating the Special Education Maze: A Guide for Parents and Teachers*. 3d ed. Bethesda, Md.: Woodbine House.

Chansky, Tamar E. 2001. *Freeing Your Child from Obsessive-Compulsive Disorder: A Powerful, Practical Program for Parents of Children and Adolescents*. New York: Three Rivers Press.

Ferber, Richard. [1985] 2004. *Solve Your Child's Sleep Problems*. Reprint. New York: Fireside.

Johnston, Hugh, and J. Jay Fruchling. 2002. *Obsessive-Compulsive Disorder in Children and Adolescents: A Guide*. Madison, Wis.: Madison Institute of Medicine.

Johnston, Hugh F., and J. Jay Fruehling. 1995. *OCD and Parenting*. Madison, Wis.: Child Psychopharmacology Information Center, University of Wisconsin (Department of Psychiatry).

Phelan, Thomas. 1996. *1-2-3 Magic: Effective Discipline for Children 2–12*. 2d rev. Ada, Mich.: Child Management.

Siegel, Lawrence M. 2001. *The Complete IEP Guide: How to Advocate for Your Special Ed Child*. Berkeley, Calif.: Nolo Press.

Swedo, Susan, and Henrietta Leonard. 1998. *Is It "Just a Phase"? How to Tell Common Childhood Phases from More Serious Problems*. New York: Golden Books.

Van Noppen, Barbara L., Michele Pato, and Steven Rasmussen. 1997. *Learning to Live with OCD, Obsessive-Compulsive Disorder*. 4th ed. Milford, Conn.: Obsessive-Compulsive Foundation.

Wagner, Aureen Pinto. 2002a. *What to Do When Your Child Has Obsessive-Compulsive Disorder: Strategies and Solutions*. Rochester, N.Y.: Lighthouse Press, Inc.

———. 2002b. *Worried No More: Help and Hope for Anxious Children*. Rochester, N.Y.: Lighthouse Press, Inc.

Waltz, Mitzi. 2000. *Obsessive-Compulsive Disorder: Help for Children and Adolescents*. Sebastopol, Calif.: O'Reilly and Associates Inc.

For Teachers

Adams, Gail B., and Marcia Torchia. 1998. *School Personnel: A Critical Link in the Identification, Treatment, and Management of OCD in Children and Adolescents*. Milford, Conn.: Obsessive-Compulsive Foundation.

Chansky, Tamar, and Jonathan B. Grayson. 1988. *Teacher's Guidelines for Helping Children with Obsessive-Compulsive Disorder in the Classroom.* Milford, Conn.: Obsessive-Compulsive Foundation.

Dornbush, Marilyn, and Sheryl Pruitt. 1993. *Teaching the Tiger: A Handbook for Individuals Involved in the Education of Students with Attention Deficit Disorders, Tourette Syndrome, or Obsessive-Compulsive Disorder.* Duarte, Calif.: Hope Press.

Multimedia Obsessive-Compulsive Foundation. 1998. *How to Recognize and Respond to OCD in School-Age Children.* Multimedia Package. Milford, Conn.: Obsessive-Compulsive Foundation.

For Therapists

Kozak, Michael, and Edna Foa. 1997. *Mastery of Obsessive Compulsive Disorder Therapist Guide.* Therapyworks Series. San Antonio, Tex.: Psychological Publications.

March, John, and Karen Mulle. 1998. *OCD in Children and Adolescents: A Cognitive-Behavioral Treatment Manual.* New York: Guilford Press.

Steketee, Gail. 1999. *Overcoming Obsessive-Compulsive Disorder: A Behavioral and Cognitive Protocol for the Treatment of OCD (Therapist Protocol).* Oakland, Calif.: New Harbinger Publications.

OCD Self-Help Books

Baer, Lee. 2000. *Getting Control: Overcoming Your Obsessions and Compulsions.* New York: Plume.

———. 2001. *The Imp of the Mind: Exploring the Silent Epidemic of Obsessive Bad Thoughts.* New York: E. P. Dutton.

Ciarrocchi, Joseph W. 1995. *The Doubting Disease: Help for Scrupulosity and Religious Compulsions.* Mahwah, N.J.: Paulist Press.

Foa, Edna B., and Reid Wilson. 2001. *Stop Obsessing! How to Overcome Your Obsessions and Compulsions.* New York: Bantam Books.

Grayson, Jonathan. 2003. *Freedom from Obsessive-Compulsive Disorder: A Personalized Recovery Program for Conquering Your Fears and Managing Disorder in Everyday Life.* New York: Tarcher/Penguin Putnam.

Hyman, Bruce M., and Cherry Pedrick. 1999. *The OCD Workbook: Your Guide to Breaking Free from Obsessive-Compulsive Disorder.* Oakland, Calif.: New Harbinger Publications.

Neziroglu, Fugen, and Jose A. Yaryura-Tobias. 1995. *Over and Over Again: Understanding Obsessive-Compulsive Disorder.* New York: Lexington Books.

Osborn, Ian. 1998. *Tormenting Thoughts and Secret Rituals: The Hidden Epidemic of Obsessive-Compulsive Disorder.* New York: Pantheon Books.

Penzel, Fred. 2000. *Obsessive-Compulsive Disorders: A Complete Guide to Getting Well and Staying Well.* New York: Oxford University Press.

Rapoport, Judith L. 1989. *The Boy Who Couldn't Stop Washing: The Experience and Treatment of Obsessive-Compulsive Disorder.* New York: E. P. Dutton.

Schwartz, Jeffrey, and Beverly Beyette. 1996. *Brain Lock: Free Yourself from Obsessive-Compulsive Behavior.* New York: ReganBooks.

Steketee, Gail, and Kerrin White. 1990. *When Once Is Not Enough: Help for Obsessive Compulsives.* Oakland, Calif.: New Harbinger Publications.

Organizations and Web Sites of Interest

Anxiety Disorders Association of America, Dept. A, 6000 Executive Blvd., Suite 513, Rockville, MD 20852. (301) 231-9350. www.adaa.org

Association for the Advancement of Behavior Therapy, 305 Seventh Avenue, New York, NY 10001-6008. (212) 647-1890. www.aabt.org

Cherry Pedrick's Web site: www.marvelite.prohosting.com/cherlene

Obsessive Action, Aberdeen Centre, 22–24 Highbury Grove, London N5 2EA. 020-7-226-4000; Fax: 020-7-288-0828. (British organization for people with OCD that offers a very informative CD-ROM, *Why Me? Obsessive-Compulsive Disorder: Information for Young People, Families, and Professionals.*)

Obsessive-Compulsive Foundation, Inc., P.O. Box 70, Milford, CT 06460-0070. (203) 878-5669. www.ocfoundation.org

Obsessive Compulsive Information Center, Madison Institute of Medicine, Inc., 7617 Mineral Point Road, Suite 300, Madison, WI 53717. (608) 827-2470. www.miminc.org

OCD Resource Center. www.ocdresource.com (Sponsored by Solvay Pharmaceuticals, this site includes "Club OCD," a special section for children, teens, and parents with information, games, and artwork.)

OCD Resource Center of South Florida. www.ocdhope.com

References

Alsobrook, John P., II, and David Pauls. 1998. Genetics of obsessive-compulsive disorder. In *Obsessive-Compulsive Disorders: Practical Management,* edited by Michael Jenike, Lee Baer, and William Minichiello. St. Louis: Mosby, Inc.

APA (American Psychiatric Association). 2000. *Diagnostic and Statistical Manual of Mental Disorders (DSM-IV-TR).* 4th ed. Text revision. Washington, D.C.: American Psychiatric Association.

Geller, Daniel A. 1998. Juvenile obsessive-compulsive disorder. In *Obsessive-Compulsive Disorders: Practical Management,* edited by Michael Jenike, Lee Baer, and William Minichiello. St. Louis: Mosby, Inc.

Grayson, Jonathan. 1996. "Do We Know Where We Are; or, Would I Have OCD in a Parallel Universe?" Paper presented at the third annual convention of the Obsessive-Compulsive Foundation, San Jose, California, September 7, 1996.

———. 1997. *G.O.A.L. Handbook: Running a Successful Support Group for OCD.* Milford, Conn.: Obsessive-Compulsive Foundation.

———. 1999. Series response: Compliance and understanding OCD. *Cognitive and Behavioral Therapy* 4:415–21.

————. 2003. *Freedom from Obsessive-Compulsive Disorder: A Personalized Recovery Program for Conquering Your Fears and Managing Uncertainty in Everyday Life.* New York: Tarcher/Penguin Putnam.

Jenike, Michael. 1998. Theories of etiology. In *Obsessive-Compulsive Disorders: Practical Management,* edited by Michael Jenike, Lee Baer, and William Minichiello. St. Louis: Mosby, Inc.

March, John, Allen Frances, Daniel Carpenter, and David A. Kahn. 1997. The Expert Consensus Guidelines Series: Treatment of obsessive-compulsive disorder. *Journal of Clinical Psychiatry* 58 (Supplement 4).

March, John, and Karen Mulle. 1998. *OCD in Children and Adolescents: A Cognitive-Behavioral Treatment Manual.* New York: Guilford Press.

Niehaus, Dana J. H., and Dan J. Stein. 1997. Obsessive-compulsive disorder: Diagnosis and assessment. In *Obsessive-Compulsive Disorders: Diagnosis, Etiology, Treatment,* edited by Eric Hollander and Dan J. Stein. New York: Dekker, Inc.

Schwartz, Jeffrey, and Beverly Beyette. 1996. *Brain Lock: Free Yourself from Obsessive-Compulsive Behavior.* New York: ReganBooks.

Wagner, Aureen Pinto. 2002. *What to Do When Your Child Has Obsessive-Compulsive Disorder: Strategies and Solutions.* Rochester, N.Y.: Lighthouse Press, Inc.

Yaryura-Tobias, Jose A., and Fugen A. Neziroglu. 1997. *Obsessive-Compulsive Disorder Spectrum: Pathogenesis, Diagnosis, and Treatment.* Washington, D.C.: American Psychiatric Press.

Lee Fitzgibbons, Ph.D., is the former director of the Children's Program at the Anxiety and Agoraphobia Treatment Center in Bala Cynwyd, Pennsylvania. She is currently in private practice in Bethlehem, New Hampshire. A professional member of the Obsessive-Compulsive Foundation and the Anxiety Disorders Association of America, she regularly presents workshops for both lay and professional audiences.

Cherry Pedrick, RN, is a registered nurse and freelance writer. In 1994, after being diagnosed with OCD, she began an intensive search for knowledge, effective treatment, and management of obsessive-compulsive disorder. She has coauthored many books for people with obsessive-compulsive spectrum disorders, including *The OCD Workbook.*

Some Other
New Harbinger Titles

The Turbulent Twenties, Item 4216 $14.95

The Balanced Mom, Item 4534 $14.95

Helping Your Child Overcome Separation Anxiety & School Refusal, Item 4313 $14.95

When Your Child Is Cutting, Item 4375 $15.95

Helping Your Child with Selective Mutism, Item 416X $14.95

Sun Protection for Life, Item 4194 $11.95

Helping Your Child with Autism Spectrum Disorder, Item 3848 $17.95

Teach Me to Say It Right, Item 4038 $13.95

Grieving Mindfully, Item 4011 $14.95

The Courage to Trust, Item 3805 $14.95

The Gift of ADHD, Item 3899 $14.95

The Power of Two Workbook, Item 3341 $19.95

Adult Children of Divorce, Item 3368 $14.95

Fifty Great Tips, Tricks, and Techniques to Connect with Your Teen, Item 3597 $10.95

Helping Your Child with OCD, Item 3325 $19.95

Helping Your Depressed Child, Item 3228 $14.95

The Couples's Guide to Love and Money, Item 3112 $18.95

50 Wonderful Ways to be a Single-Parent Family, Item 3082 $12.95

Caring for Your Grieving Child, Item 3066 $14.95

Helping Your Child Overcome an Eating Disorder, Item 3104 $16.95

Helping Your Angry Child, Item 3120 $19.95

The Stepparent's Survival Guide, Item 3058 $17.95

Drugs and Your Kid, Item 3015 $15.95

The Daughter-In-Law's Survival Guide, Item 2817 $12.95

Whose Life Is It Anyway?, Item 2892 $14.95

It Happened to Me, Item 2795 $21.95

Act it Out, Item 2906 $19.95

Parenting Your Older Adopted Child, Item 2841 $16.95

Boy Talk, Item 271X $14.95

Talking to Alzheimer's, Item 2701 $12.95

Helping a Child with Nonverbal Learning Disorder or Asperger's Syndrome, Item 2779 $14.95

When Anger Hurts Your Relationship, Item 2604 $13.95

Call **toll free, 1-800-748-6273,** or log on to our online bookstore at **www.newharbinger.com** to order. Have your Visa or Mastercard number ready. Or send a check for the titles you want to New Harbinger Publications, Inc., 5674 Shattuck Ave., Oakland, CA 94609. Include $4.50 for the first book and 75¢ for each additional book, to cover shipping and handling. (California residents please include appropriate sales tax.) Allow two to five weeks for delivery.

Prices subject to change without notice.